Poetic Faith

Various Topics and Biblical Doctrines Explored, Discussed, and then Put to Rhyme

RANDY MLEJNEK

ISBN 978-1-63575-839-9 (Paperback)
ISBN 978-1-64079-169-5 (Hard Cover)
ISBN 978-1-63575-840-5 (Digital)

Christian Faith Publishing, Inc.
296 Chestnut Street
Meadville, PA 16335
www.christianfaithpublishing.com

Printed in the United States of America

To the love of my life, my best friend, and my beautiful bride, my
wife Amanda. Without her constant love
and support, this work would
not have been possible. I love you ARM
and I thank my God upon every
remembrance of you.
5013

To my mother, Glenda Mlejnek, thank you for leading me
to Christ as a young boy. Thank you for taking me to church
when I was growing up and for your unceasing prayer for
me over the years. You have always believed in me and God
truly blessed me with such a wonderful mother in you.

I also dedicate this book in loving memory
to my Mother in Law, Debbie
Mills. To whom, I owe a special debt of gratitude. She strongly
encouraged me to share my writings with the world.

Introduction

I would describe this book as a combination devotional, Christian living guide, and topical Bible study. My book adheres to the mantra that variety is the spice of life. It takes the reader on a religious roller coaster, diving in to a diverse doctrinal melting pot put to poetry. It examines many different modern-day issues and topics as they relate to biblical faith.

I believe this book may be a good resource to many who are interested in Christian, religious, and spiritually themed literature. I believe its content to be both timely and timeless. It is one of those books that people can read, reread, and often refer back to as the different topics become relevant in their lives. It covers a wide range of topics viewed through the lens of a biblical perspective and worldview. It also happens to be extremely unique in its composition. One of the unique things about this book, is that it incorporates an original artistic component by closing each chapter with a poem that I have written, that directly relates to the topic being discussed.

Its topics encompass many areas of interest, including prophecy, God's design for sex and marriage, abortion, heaven, angels, spiritual warfare, the Holy Spirit, prayer, temptation as well as the incarnation, crucifixion, resurrection of Jesus, and many more. I also included some short personal stories that convey lessons that I've learned along the way in my own journey of faith.

I

Does God Give Us More than We Can Handle?

I've heard this phrase used so many times and not just in religious circles either. I'm sure that you have heard it a number of times as well, or maybe you have even used it yourself. It is usually given out in an attempt to encourage someone who is going through a difficult struggle in their life. I've heard regular church-attending Christians offer this sentiment to someone in the midst of great suffering. They will say, "Remember, God will never give you more than you can handle or that you are able to bear." This intended comfort is given with confidence, as if it was taken directly from the pages of the scriptures. So let's briefly examine this common cliché and see how its wisdom lines up with the Word of God. That, ultimately, should be our test for all things as Christians.

There is a verse in the New Testament that some will point to when trying to justify this statement and to try to give it authority. It is found in 1 Corinthians 10:13. It says, "No temptation has overtaken you except such as is common to man; but God *is* faithful, who will not allow you to be tempted beyond what you are able, but with the temptation will also make the way of escape, that you may be able to bear *it*" (NKJV). This verse is talking about temptation, not trials.

God will never allow you to be tempted to sin, as a Christian, beyond your ability to be able to resist that temptation and He is faithful to provide a way of escape for the temptation. This verse then gets mis-quoted and taken out of context to support this unbiblical wisdom.

There is no promise in the Bible where God tells us that we will never be given more than we can handle. In fact, the Bible is filled with examples where people were given more than they could handle. If you look at the life of David, Elijah, and Moses, you will see many times where they were given more than they could handle. So why does God allow us to be given more than we can handle at times? There are several main reasons for this, I believe. One of the obvious ones would be that if we could handle everything life throws our way on our own, then what would we need God's help for?

God, sometimes, allows us to be given more than we can handle to teach us that we need to trust, depend, and rely fully upon Him. Jesus said that apart from Him, we could do nothing (John 15:5). The Christian life is not meant to be lived by our own strength and power. God wants our full reliance and trust to be upon Him. We are given more than we can handle so that our faith can grow and we can learn to surrender to His will and way in our lives. When we try to do things in our own strength, that is when we run into trouble. I'm guilty of this so often myself. I try to pick up and carry burdens that are not mine to bear in my own power. That's why 1 Peter 5:7 says to cast our cares and anxieties upon Him for He cares for us. We are told to be strong in the Lord and in the power of *His* might (Eph. 6:10). We are given more than we can handle so that God's presence and power can be made known and manifested in our lives.

When, in our pride, we think that we can handle things better our way, on our own, we usually fall flat on our face. "Pride goes before destruction, and a haughty spirit before a fall" (Prov. 16:18, ESV). We need to trust in the Shepherd and be sensitive to His lead-ing. This involves maintaining daily, close, and intimate contact with

Him. If you want to hear the Shepherd's voice, you need to be following Him closely and walking obediently after Him. This involves a total reliance and dependence upon Him to realize that without Him, we are nothing. To understand this, let's look at what this old song says: "I can't even walk without Him holding my hand." As 1 Chronicles 16:11 says, we are to continually seek the Lord's face.

The apostle Paul writing to the church at Corinth in 2 Corinthians 1:8 said that he and other followers of Jesus experienced trials and troubles that were "far beyond our ability to endure" (NIV). Then, in verse 9 he says, "…But this happened that we might not rely on ourselves but on God…" That is the lesson right there—that we will face trials, suffering, pain, and difficulties in this life that will be too great for us to endure *on our own.*

I am given more than I can handle all the time. I have to remember that when I am weak, He is strong. His strength is made perfect in weakness (2 Cor. 12:9). No matter what trials or storms that you may face, if you trust in the Lord, you will learn that His grace is sufficient for you. I've heard it said that sometimes, God calms the raging storms in our life, and other times, He allows the storm to continue to rage and He calms us. He can give the peace that passes all understanding (Phil. 4:7), and He can give you joy even in the midst of the most difficult of sufferings. I like the saying, "If you put everything in God's hands, you will see God's hands in everything." Remember Matthew 11:28: "Come to me, all you who are weary and burdened, and I will give you rest" (NIV).

Are you in the eye of a storm in your life right now? My family and I are going through a very difficult trial of our own now that came right on the heels of a previous trial. They are both more than we can handle and are able to bear by our own strength. We have found that His grace has been sufficient every step of the way. Maybe you are overwhelmed with what you have on your plate at the moment and with the particular difficulty you might be facing?

Remember to keep your eyes focused and fixed on Jesus and not the storm that is raging around you. Keep in mind the story of when Jesus walked on the water and Peter stepped out of the boat in faith and began to walk toward Jesus on the water too. Then, Peter took his eyes off of the Lord and began to doubt and looked at the wind and waves and began to sink. Don't try to handle it by your own power and don't take your eyes off the Savior.

I close this chapter with a poem that I wrote about this topic. I pray that it will be an encouragement and a blessing to you today.

Does God Give Us More than We Can Handle?

There is an often repeated phrase used that
is meant to be a comforting cliché.
As students of the Word, we must ask ourselves,
what does the Bible actually say?
The saying states, "God will not give you more than
you can handle or that you are able to bear."
You might feel confident that this statement can be
found in the Bible, but you would be in error.
This comes from 1st Corinthians 10:13, being taken
out of context and is a tragic misquotation.
This passage of the scripture does not refer to trials,
pain, or suffering, rather to temptation.
God will not allow you to be tempted by anything
greater than your ability to be able to resist.
He is faithful and provides an escape to bear it; it's
this verse that people misquote and twist
The truth is we are, at times, given more than we
can bear to help us to surrender and to grow,
To keep us moving forward, pressing toward the
mark when we've reached a spiritual plateau.
Never facing more than we can handle, God would
be unnecessary; we could make it on our own.
So He teaches us that we need to depend upon Him
by moving us outside our comfort zone.
As we learn to rely on Him, we will see that His
strength is made perfect when we are weak.
We can't live the Christian life by our own power;
it's *His* face that we need to continually seek
When life's storms become overwhelming and the
road you are on seems impossibly rough,

11

Realize that some burdens are not yours to carry
alone; you are simply not strong enough.
Take comfort in knowing that through every
trial and in every situation that you face,
When you fully trust in Christ, you will discover
the sufficiency of His amazing grace.
When life knocks you down and robs you of sleep
while you burn both ends of the candle,
Cast all your cares upon Him, for God will never
give you more than *He* can handle.

Randy Mlejnek

2

Temptation

They say that the eyes are the windows to the soul. I believe that it is very important to be careful of what we put in front of our eyes. Once you look at something, it can never be unseen. Pornography is a multibillion dollar a year industry, and it has been said that it is more addictive than heroin or crack cocaine. In today's digital age, it is more readily and privately available than ever before. It can ruin lives, marriages, and cause a great amount of damage both to those who participate in it and to those who watch it. It objectifies women and abuses and perverts the gift of sex that God gave to us. I know that according to God's Word, it says that the eyes are never fully satisfied (Prov. 27:20). The lustful greed and sinful desires of human beings are never fully met. Yes, you may find temporary satisfaction, and there is pleasure in sin for a season (Heb. 11:25). But at the end of the day, it will leave you even emptier than before.

We need to be so careful of what we allow our eyes to see, and that applies to many things, not just pornography. We need to be careful of the movies and television shows that we watch and the books and magazines that we read. What you look at will affect what you think about. There is an old saying that states, "Sow a thought, reap an action. Sow an action, reap a habit. Sow a habit, reap a character. Sow a character, reap a destiny." The Bible says that we will reap what we sow (Gal. 6:7). So be careful of what you allow your eyes to see.

Not only do we need to be careful of what we look at, but also what we listen to, the places that we go, the things that we do, and the words that we speak. There is a song I used to sing as a kid in church that said, "O, be careful, little eyes, what you see. O, be careful, little ears, what you hear. O, be careful, little hands, what you do. O, be careful, little feet, where you go. O, be careful, little mouth, what you say. There's a Father up above, and He's looking down in love. So be careful, little eyes, what you see…" I wrote a poem based loosely off that concept. I titled it *Be Careful*, and it will be at the end of this chapter for you to read.

This is an important biblical principle—that we, as Christians, need to be careful how we live our lives. He called us to be holy as He is holy (1 Pet. 1:15–16). God gave us free will and the ability to make our own choices. We are free to make our own choices, but we are not free from the consequences of those choices. The temptation to do things that are morally wrong and contrary to God's Word is ever present. Paul said that in his flesh dwells no good thing (Rom. 7:18). We are sinful beings. The world's wisdom today tells us to do whatever feels good or makes us happy. That truth is relative and ethics depend on the situation. We are told that the Bible is an outdated book, and it is clearly seen that the biblical Christian worldview is not very popular today. We, as Christians, need to be ever vigilant because our adversary, the devil, walks about as a roaring lion, seeking whom he may devour (1 Pet. 5:8). We need to walk in the Spirit so that we will not fulfill the lusts of the flesh (Gal. 5:16).

Temptation can come in the form of any number of poisonous, sinful vices that can cause you untold misery, pain, loss, and ultimately destroy your soul. Pornography, drunkenness, drugs, fornication, adultery, the love of money, greed, pride, lust, covetousness, gluttony, et cetera. That list could go on and on. Make no mistake about it, though; your enemy knows exactly which flavor of sin to bait his hook with for you.

I don't remember where I first heard this next phrase, but it is so true. There is a God-shaped hole in our heart that can only be filled by Him. Trying to fill that hole with anything other than God will leave you completely empty and lost. C.S. Lewis said, "God designed the human machine to run on himself. He himself is the fuel that our spirits were designed to burn and the food our spirits were designed to feed on, there is no other." We get so wrapped up in this life, what it has to offer, and living in the here and now that we don't think about eternity. It is so important to be careful of what we look at, what we listen to, what we say, where we go, and what we do.

Jesus willingly laid down His very life according to the Father's sovereign will. He died for us, but we are called to present our bodies as living sacrifices for Him (Rom. 12:1). We have to be willing to die every single day to our own sinful desires in order to completely follow Him. We have to be willing to lose our life for His sake in order to truly find it. This is much easier said than done. The thing about being a living sacrifice is that, sometimes, we tend to want to get up and climb down off of that altar. What was the example Jesus gave to us when He was tempted by the devil in the wilderness? He responded by quoting scripture to him. I think that is one of the greatest examples that we could follow. We need to saturate and immerse ourselves in the Word of God. "Thy word have I hid in mine heart that I might not sin against thee" (Ps. 119:11).

Be Careful

Be careful what you put before your eyes and allow them to see.
That vision can't be taken back, and it gets stored in your memory.
Don't give in to your sin to feed your lust and greed.
The eyes are never satisfied; you'll never fill that need.
Be careful, my friend, what things that you allow your ears to hear.
Not all sounds are harmless, and their consequences can be severe.
Be careful what you put effort into and allow your hands to do.
Left idle, they can be used in a workshop to give the devil his due.
Be careful where your feet take you and
where you allow yourself to go,
And be not deceived. God will not be
mocked; you will reap what you sow.
Be careful in your choice of words, and
measure exactly what you will say.
Like a bullet fired, they can't be taken back;
you can't stop them halfway.
Temptation comes to all of us, and eventually,
it will knock on your door.
Stand strong in the Lord, and be careful
what you acquire a taste for.
In a day when sex sells and personal pleasure is taken to the extreme,
Fight against the raging current, and be
that one that swims upstream.
We're told that morals and truth are relative
and ethics depend on the situation.
Don't buy into those lies; they run counter to
God's Word and lead to damnation.
Satan is a master deceiver; he shows you
the bait while he hides the hook.

Ask God for strength; resist his enticing
traps, for he is a liar and a crook.
Because once that sin takes hold and the devil's hook has been set,
Your will—it seems—is not your own, and
you will suffer pain and regret.
Once that sin becomes a habit, your conscience can become seared.
No longer having to be tempted, you will have simply volunteered.
This fishing trip is not one where you get to
relax when from this life you retire.
The stakes are eternal, the consequences are
real, and the lake is made of fire.
Realize that the devil is the one fishing, and
you are actually the catch on his pole.
Be careful; he's not just after your mind and
your body but, ultimately, your soul.

Randy Mlejnek

3

Loose Lips Sink Ships

Sticks and stones may break my bones, but words will never hurt me. Such a well-known phrase that has been around for a very long time. We all learned it at a young age and also discovered along the way that it was a complete lie. Words *can* hurt! Words can cut to the very core of a person as well as any blade. Words can break a heart in a thousand pieces. Words can destroy someone's good reputation, his or her career, or his or her very livelihood in an instant. Gossip, slander, and lies can sever lifelong friendships, break up marriages, ruin a business, or cause a church to split. It is important to remember that once something is said, it can never be taken back. Your words may be able to be forgiven, but they will never be forgotten.

Words are important, and what you say matters. Your words can be used to give encouragement and support or to tear someone down. The Bible says that one day, we will have to give an account for every careless or idle word that we have spoken (Matt. 12:36). Your words can be potent and powerful. They can be used for good or for evil. The Bible says that death and life are in the power of the tongue (Prov. 18:21). Yes, words can literally be deadly. A false witness in a court of law can cause someone to be put to death unjustly. Many teenagers have committed suicide because of the unrelenting teasing, mocking, and words of humiliation from their peers. Words have started wars and helped spread the message and propaganda of evil dictators; think of Hitler for example.

You can also use your words to bring hope and to lift others up. You can say something helpful, motivational, and encouraging to someone that can change the very course of their life. The Bible says that a word fitly spoken is like apples of gold in settings of silver (Prov. 25:11). Words can be beautiful, but they can also be ugly. The Bible says not to allow any corrupt communication to proceed out of your mouth, but that which is good… (Eph. 4:29). God's Word says that the tongue is an unruly evil, full of deadly poison that no man can tame (James 3:8). And Proverbs 12:18 says, "The words of the reckless pierce like swords, but the tongue of the wise brings healing" (NIV).

God's Word has much to say about the tongue and our words. It says in Matthew 12:34, "…For out of the abundance of the heart the mouth speaks." If you want to know what is truly in a man's heart, just listen to what comes out of his mouth. James 1:26 tells us that if people consider themselves religious but don't keep a tight rein on their tongue, they deceive themselves, and their religion is worthless. "Just as a nurse puts a thermometer under your tongue and tells your physical temperature. James says your tongue itself will reveal your spiritual temperature," John MacArthur Jr.

Words can be used to ask for or give forgiveness. They can also destroy another person and cause them such emotional harm that can deeply scar and stay with them for a lifetime. The book of James talks about how a great forest can be set ablaze by such a small fire. Spreading just a little bit of "harmless" gossip can be the spark that starts a raging inferno that, in turn, burns someone's life to the ground. Don't be the spark that starts that blaze by spreading gossip or the fuel for that fire (listening ears) to help it spread.

James uses a couple of other analogies to drive home his point about the importance of controlling your tongue. He mentions how a horse is controlled with a small bit that is put in its mouth, how such a large and powerful animal can be controlled with a tiny bit pressing against its tongue. He also mentions how such a big ship can be turned about with such a tiny rudder. Just as the tongue is such a small part of our body but what it produces (words) can have such a huge impact, control, and influence on our lives and on the lives of those around us. Words are important; it is what God used to communicate His truth to us (John 1:1).

Are you careful with your words? Do you think before you speak? In other words—and I found this advice on the Internet—try *tasting* those words first before you spit them out. My advice is to ask yourself these questions before you speak: Are your words used to support or separate, to motivate or manipulate, to bless or blaspheme, to be constructive or critical, to hurt or heal, to help or harass, to be prudent or perverse? Are your words delicate and decent or destructive and deceitful? James 1:19 says to be quick to listen, slow to speak, and slow to become angry. I think those are great words to live by. I've heard it said that since God gave us two ears and one mouth, maybe we should listen twice as much as we speak? Seems like good advice to me. The Bible does say that in a multitude of words, sin is not lacking (Prov. 10:19). Sometimes, being quiet and holding our peace is the best option. Better to keep quiet and let them think that you are wise than to open your mouth and remove all doubt. Proverbs 17:28 speaks of this.

"Words are seeds that do more than blow around. They land in our hearts and not the ground. Be careful what you plant and careful what you say. You might have to eat what you planted one day" (Unknown).

"Every one of us is carrying around a concealed weapon. All we have to do is open our mouths and it's unconcealed" (Unknown).

Just as a gun can be used for good or evil, the same goes for the tongue, and once you fire that bullet, you can't take it back. How do you use your concealed weapon? Are you ultracritical and judgmental of others with your words? There are two simple words that many people seem so hesitant to say. Even though we do not like the taste of it, sometimes, we just need to eat that slice of humble pie and say those two words: "I'm sorry." There have been so many times that I have withheld those words out of my own stubbornness and pride. We don't like to admit when we are wrong and have caused someone hurt or loss. Is there anyone that you need to apologize to today?

How about you, Christian, have you been guilty of using your words for gossip lately? By the way, I think listening to it is just as bad as spreading it. Keep in mind that it has been said that those that gossip to you will probably also gossip about you. Don't be the fuel that helps spread that fire. Proverbs 16:28 states, "A dishonest man spreads strife, and a whisperer separates close friends" (ESV). I need to take my own words to heart from this chapter, I'm guilty of these things. I tend to be critical, judgmental, and like to listen to gossip. It is a difficult habit to break.

I read a fair amount, and I came across a good three question approach to help measure our words. I wish I could remember where I read this to give them credit, but I apologize I don't. It goes along with remembering to think before you speak. The first question asks, "will these words I'm about to say help or harm?" Number two asks, "am I trying to retaliate or restore?" And number three asks, "am I pursuing peace or punishing?" I think that those are great questions to ask ourselves before we respond to someone. There is another old adage that goes like this: "If you don't have anything nice to say, don't say anything at all." I think I like that one better than the "sticks and stones" one. I close this chapter out with a poem that I wrote about the tongue.

The Tongue

It is small and full of deadly poison that no man can tame,
And it only takes a little spark to grow into a giant flame.
Just as a tiny rudder has the ability to control a massive ship.
Your words can negatively affect and sting like the crack of a whip.
Your tongue can be used to give a blessing or to give a curse,
To grant forgiveness or to take a situation from bad to worse.
Once a word has been spoken, it can never be taken back.
Think before you speak, and know that what
you say, God is keeping track.
Someday, you will give an account for every
idle word that you have spoken,
For the damage that your words have caused
and the lives they have broken.
If you never acknowledge your creator or of His majesty profess,
The fact that Jesus Christ is Lord, one
day, every tongue will confess.
Do not allow any corrupt communication
to proceed from your lips.
Slander and gossip can destroy a reputation
like a knife slashes and rips.
You cannot draw both bitter and fresh water from the same well.
Wondering if a man's religion is real, by his words you can tell.
For out of the abundance of the heart the mouth does speak,
And though it be little, it is amazing at the havoc it can wreak.
Even a fool who holds his peace will be counted as wise.
Be slow to speak and quick to listen—
that's what the Bible does advise
So be careful what you say as death and life
are in the power of the tongue.

This is a very valuable lesson and one best
learned while you are young.

Randy Mlejnek

4

Biblical Faith: A Closer Look

The Christian faith is not a blind faith, wishful thinking, or leap in the dark—far from it. It is reasonable, logical, and full of very convincing evidence. The truth is right there in front of our eyes, contained in the Bible for all to see and examine. If one were to honestly and openly sift through and investigate the scriptures, the evidence is clear and convincing.

I just got done reading the book *Cold-Case Christianity* by J. Warner Wallace (as featured in the recently released movie *God's Not Dead 2*), and I highly recommend it! A real life, highly trained, cold-case homicide detective and former devout atheist examines the evidences for Christianity, utilizing the same modern methods he uses in his law enforcement investigations. He became a Christian through this investigation. There have been numerous books written by former atheists who have become Christians after thoroughly investigating the claims of the Bible—books that detail the evidence they uncovered. *More than a Carpenter* by Josh McDowell and *The Case for Christ* by Lee Strobel are just a couple of other examples.

"Faith is Trusting in which you have good reason
to think is true" (William Lane Craig).

Yet critics and skeptics of Christianity will say that there is not enough evidence. They are looking for evidence beyond any shadow of a doubt whatsoever. They seem to want high definition, full-color, 1080p video footage of the biblical accounts from multiple viewing angles. They want evidence that removes any possibility of any other explanation to the point of being beyond coercive. In other words, evidence that removes the need for faith.

The problem is that in Christianity, faith is not optional. It is absolutely essential. The Bible says that without faith, it is impossible to please God (Heb. 11:6). Ephesians 2:8–9 says, "For by grace are ye saved *through faith,* and that not of yourselves it is the gift of God, not of works, lest any man should boast" (KJV). The evidence is available to all of us. Some people just choose to suppress the truth of God and exchange it for a lie (Rom. 1).

"God doesn't force himself upon us. He has given evidence of Himself which is sufficiently clear for those with an open mind and an open heart, but sufficiently vague so as not to compel those whose hearts are closed" (William Lane Craig).

The French mathematical genius Blaise Pascal said, "Willing to appear openly to those who see him with all their heart, and to be hidden from those who flee from him with all their heart, God so regulates the knowledge of himself that he has given indications of himself which are visible to those who seek him and not to those who do not seek him. There is enough light for those to see who only desire to see, and enough obscurity for those who have a contrary disposition."

Sincerity is also not the full measure of true biblical faith. There are a lot of people who are sincere in what they believe; unfortunately, many of them are sincerely wrong. It has been said that the road to hell is paved with sincerity. Faith is only as good as the object in which it is placed. How reliable and trustworthy is the object of your faith?

So what then is faith? Hebrews 11:1 says, "Now faith is the substance of things hoped for, the evidence of things not seen" (KJV). The Bible tells us that we are supposed to walk by faith and not by sight (2 Cor. 5:7) and that the just and the righteous shall live by faith (Hab. 2:4, Heb. 10:38). Faith is putting your trust and reliance in the finished work of Jesus Christ and His death, burial, and resurrection. It is that blessed assurance that "Jesus is mine" like the old hymn states. It is not a "hope so" faith, but a rock solid "know so," "for sure" faith. 1 John 5:13 says, "I write these things to you who believe in the name of the Son of God that you may *know* that you have eternal life" (ESV). I like the following acronym for the word *faith* that I think describes it clearly.

*F*inding

*A*ssurance

*I*n

*T*rusting

*H*im

There is a popular story that I think helps illustrate, in a way, the concept of saving faith in Christ. It is about an amazing tightrope walker by the name of Charles Blondin. On June 30, 1859, he became the first man to walk on a tightrope across Niagara Falls—1,100 feet across suspended 160 feet above the deadly flow of water. He did this with no harness or safety net. He walked back and forth many times. Once, he even walked across on stilts. He even pushed a wheelbarrow across with a heavy load in it. He spotted a man cheering in the crowd and asked him if he thought that he could safely carry him across in the wheelbarrow. The man said yes. To which Blondin replied with a smile, "Get in." The man declined the offer.

It is one thing to believe that he could walk across by himself, yet another thing to believe that he could safely carry you across. It is another thing entirely to trust in and rely totally on him to get you across by actually getting in the wheelbarrow. With Jesus, it is more than mere mental assent and believing a set of historical facts about Him as recorded in the scriptures. It is exercising that faith by putting your complete trust, dependence, confidence, and reliance in Him to save your soul and carry you home. It is not so much the amount of our faith as it is the object of our faith that makes it an effective saving faith. There are many people who have faith in things that can't save them from their sin. It is only Jesus, however, who can save you. John 14:6 says, "Jesus said to him, 'I am the way, the truth, and the life. No one comes to the Father except through Me'" (NKJV).

The Bible also says that faith without works is dead (James 2:17). Now, don't get confused; there is no contradiction there. Your works do not save you. "Not by works of righteousness which we have done, but according to his mercy he saved us..." (Titus 3:5). They are only an outward evidence or proof of a genuine faith. The Bible says that a genuine faith will produce good works. If you are truly a born-again child of God, there will be some evidence of it in your life. I don't do nice things for my wife like buy her flowers or write her poems to *be* married to her; I do those things because I *am* married to her. We don't do good works to be saved; we do good works because we are saved. Salvation is not a result of good works; good works are a result of salvation.

I don't know what's truly in your heart; only God does. But I do know that the Bible tells us that if you are a born-again child of the King, you are a "new creation" (2 Cor. 5:17). Again, there should be some fruit or evidence that you produce. The Bible says that "by their fruits you will know them" (Matt. 7:20). So I may not be able to look into your heart, but I can look at your life. I can be a "fruit inspector" so to speak. Are you bearing any fruit for God?

"If you were accused of being a Christian and put on trial for it, would there be enough evidence to convict you?" – Unknown

A discussion on biblical faith just wouldn't be complete without at least mentioning Hebrews 11. It is known as the great "Hall of Faith" chapter of the Bible. It is a list of biblical characters that put their faith into action. "By faith" precedes the descriptions of how they exercised their faith. It lists a number of biblical personalities who, by their faith, were justified by God—some of the more notable mentioned being Abraham, Moses, Noah, Sarah, Rahab, Samson, Isaac, Jacob, and Joseph.

A genuine faith will endure, and he that began a good work in you will perform it until the day of Jesus Christ (Phil. 1:6). That is not to say that we won't ever mess up or "backslide" on God. I like what I heard a wise old retired pastor at my church say not too long ago. He said, "A faith that fizzles before the finish was flawed from the first." Jesus told His disciples that if they had faith as a grain of mustard seed, they could move mountains (Matt. 17:20). What impossible situation (mountain) are you facing today? Remember, nothing is impossible with God (Luke 1:37) and that faith comes by hearing and hearing by the Word of God (Rom. 10:17).

"Faith does not eliminate the questions, but it knows where to take them" (Elisabeth Elliot).

I gave you a mental picture of saving faith with the illustration of the tightrope walker and the wheelbarrow. Although the comparison is not perfect, I think it paints a fairly clear portrait of the concept. Now, I want to take faith and dissect it a bit to look at its anatomy. What makes up the components, if you will, of faith? If you study this subject for yourself, you will probably discover that many theologians have described faith using three Latin words. They are *notitia* (knowledge), *assensus* (assent), and *fiducia* (trust). They call these the three essential elements of saving faith. Although there has been debate about these three elements and their role as they are related to faith, I think they provide us with a good description of true biblical saving faith. You can find these three essential elements of faith described in detail in many books and all over the Internet. I will try to articulate them to you from my understanding of the things that I have read.

The first element is *notitia*. It is a knowledge of the basic information. Put another way, it is the content of faith. There has to be content to faith. The message, material, substance, ingredients, or elements that constitute and make up that knowledge. You cannot have faith in nothing. So from a biblical faith standpoint, the content would be the Gospel. It would be, specifically, the death, burial, and bodily resurrection of Jesus Christ.

The second element is *assensus* (assent). It is giving intellectual credence that the content is factually true. To simply have knowledge (*notitia*) is not enough. There must be, to a certain extent, a firmly held belief that the content is factually correct and true. Where *notitia* would state the message of the Gospel, *assensus* involves giving agreement or being persuaded that the Gospel is actually historically true. These two elements or aspects of faith by themselves are not enough to constitute saving faith. There is still one element remaining.

Mental assent is a part of it, but it is not the only part. Having a head knowledge about a set of facts about Jesus and accepting it as true, (mere mental assent alone) is not saving faith. The Bible says that even the demons believe and tremble (James 2:19). You see, a lot of people miss heaven by about eighteen inches. That is the average distance between the human head and heart. True biblical saving faith requires not just a head knowledge but a *heart* acceptance too. It is a trust and a placing of reliance in the object (Jesus) of your faith.

That brings us to the third element of saving faith, which is *fiducia* (trust). This involves trust. This is actually trusting in and resting upon Jesus and the truth of the Gospel (getting in the wheelbarrow). We possess the information (*notitia*); we are convinced it is actually true (*assensus*). Now, we have to trust (*fiducia*). *Fiducia* is personal trust and reliance upon Jesus and His atoning work of the Gospel as the payment for our sins—a volitional act of your free will to accept God's gift of salvation. Fiducia goes beyond the first two elements, but they are interrelated, built upon each other, and are all necessary for saving faith.

These three elements together constitute true biblical saving faith. Just to reiterate, it is all of God and His grace. Even our faith is a gift of His grace. Remember Ephesians 2:8–9: "…We are saved by grace, through faith, and that *not of yourselves*, it is the gift of God, not of works, lest any man should boast or brag." We can't earn it; we can't buy it. It is all by God's grace, and faith is the channel through which that grace flows. *Sola fide* (justification by faith alone) is it. Faith alone—not faith plus works, or faith plus baptism, or faith plus anything else. "The only thing that we contribute to our salvation is the sin that made it necessary" (Johnathan Edwards).

> *"When a train goes through a tunnel and it gets dark,*
> *you don't throw away the ticket and jump off. You sit still*
> *and TRUST the engineer" (Corrie Ten Boom).*

Have you put your faith and trust in Him? Are you as assured of heaven as if you were already there? Have you gotten into the *wheelbarrow*? Remember, you can't get across on your own; it can't be done. Our sin separated us from God, and that divide can never be traversed on our own. Only the cross of Christ bridges that gap. Your good works won't get you there, neither will baptism, church membership, charitable giving, fame, money, power, possessions, or prestige. What are you trusting in today? Do you have biblical faith?

I close this chapter out with a poem that I wrote on the topic of faith. I pray that you will find it encouraging and that it points you to my Savior, Jesus Christ.

Faith

The Bible says we must walk by faith and not by sight.
It is not a leap into the dark but a step into the light.
Rest assured true biblical faith is not blind.
It is reason, logic, and truth all combined.
There is more to it than mere intellectual assent.
It involves trust, reliance, and a need to repent.
It's given to us by God, and without faith, it is impossible to please Him.
It is not ignorance, wishful thinking, or going out on a spiritual limb.
It is the substance of things hoped for, the evidence of things not seen.
It's not a religion; it's a relationship with God's Son, the Nazarene.
So then, faith cometh by hearing and hearing by God's Word.
Through it, the righteousness of Christ to you is transferred.
It's being sure of our hope, not hoping that it is sure.
With a solid conviction, true faith stands the test; it will endure.
You could move a mountain with faith as a grain of mustard seed.
Miracles are possible with persistent prayer for God to intercede.
Great biblical examples of it can be found in Hebrews chapter 11,
Where it is said that "by faith" those listed are assured of heaven.
Genuine faith will produce fruit, and James
says without works, it is dead.
Those works do not save you, only Jesus
and the blood that He shed.
By God's grace, through faith, we accept and believe.
That is the only way that eternal life we can receive.
Faith is only as good as the object in which it is placed.
Unless you put it in Jesus, it has surely gone to waste.

Randy Mlejnek

5

Let's Talk about Sex: A Biblical Perspective

Let's just be honest; we live in a sex-saturated, sex-crazed, and sex-obsessed culture today. We are bombarded and inundated with messages of sex and sensuality at every turn. It seems that sex is a primary part of the plot of virtually every television sitcom today. It is plastered all over billboards along the highway and in practically every popular magazine or book read today. You almost can't watch even a television commercial without some type of at least indirect reference to sex. It's in the forefront of our movies, music, magazines, media, and our minds.

Why is this? Because we live in a world of instant gratification, situational ethics, and moral relativism, and the popular mindset is that if it feels good, then do it. We put our feelings at the top place of pre-eminence in our lives as the supreme authority. Anyone who claims that there is an unchanging objective biblical moral standard is laughed at in today's world. We are obsessed with sex, and because of that obsession, sex sells. Sex is used in advertising to sell things that don't have anything to do with sex. This is why you will see a commercial, trying to sell you toothpaste with a scantily clad attractive woman in the ad with a seductive look on her face.

Sex is not a dirty word or a bad thing. It is a beautiful gift created and given to us by God and to be enjoyed. With that beautiful gift, however, was given to us boundaries and limitations on its use. It is to take place only within the proper place and context that it was designed to be enjoyed. That place is only within the committed covenantal union relationship of a husband and his wife in marriage. We, as a society, have perverted this special gift from God and accepted a cheap counterfeit in its place.

When I was a teenager attending Freedom Baptist High School in Hudsonville, Michigan, God's gift of sex to us was explained to me with an illustration using a fireplace. The fireplace is the proper place for fire. When you have a nice fire going in the fireplace, it can provide warmth, comfort, beauty, and security. If, however, you take the fire out of the fireplace, out of its proper context, disaster and destruction can occur. If you take that fire out of the boundaries where it was meant to be enjoyed and place it on the living room carpet, you can have dire consequences and possibly even burn down your house. It is the same way with sex. God created and gave sex to us to be enjoyed, for pleasure, procreation, to strengthen the bond in a relationship—but only within the context and boundaries of a marriage. First Corinthians 6:18 tells us that all other sins a person commits are outside the body, but whoever sins sexually, sins against their own body.

So why did God create something so wonderful, good, enjoyable, and then confine it only to the parameters of the marital union? It was for our own good. God did not create sex to just be a casual expression of intimacy and lust between just any two people who wanted to indulge in it. Having sex is about becoming "one flesh." Jesus said that he made them at the beginning male and female and that "for this reason a man shall leave his father and mother and be joined to his wife, and the two shall become one flesh" (Gen. 1:27, 2:24; Matt. 19:4–5). These passages of scripture clearly state that sex is reserved exclusively for marriage. In a nutshell, however, biblical marriage is to be between one man and one woman only. This was instituted by God in Genesis 2:24 and reiterated by Jesus in Matthew 19:4–5 and other parallel passages.

So God created the institution of marriage (which is why He alone gets to define it) and then sex to be enjoyed within the confines of that union only. The concept of the two becoming one flesh coincides with the apostle Paul's warning in 1 Corinthians 6:16 of not joining yourself to a prostitute. We are told not just to avoid sexual immorality, but to *flee* from it. Sexual immorality is one of the only things the Bible tells us that can be so damaging, we are not just to abstain, but to run (not walk) from it! Then, in the seventh chapter of 1 Corinthians, Paul makes clear that marriage is the only God-ordained relationship to guard against sexual immorality.

"Sex is supposed to be a marital privilege, not an audition for dating" (Unknown).

The Greek word that is used throughout the New Testament that describes fornication is the word *porneia*. It is where we get our English word for pornography. Many Bible translations translate that word into English as sexual immorality or fornication. The Bible is crystal clear in many passages that *porneia* is prohibited and sinful. It is a broad word that basically refers to all forms of illicit sexual activity outside of a marital relationship. This would include premarital sex, extramarital sex, adultery, fornication, etc.

Hebrews 13:4 tells us that the marriage bed is undefiled but that God will judge the sexually immoral (fornicators) and adulterers. In the Song of Solomon, we are told three times not to arouse or awaken love until the proper time [which is marriage] (2:7, 3:5, 8:4). Ephesians 5:3 instructs us not to have even a hint of sexual immorality among us or any kind of impurity. "Flee from sexual immorality"

(1 Cor. 6:18, NIV). "It is God's will that you should be sanctified: that you should avoid sexual immorality; that each of you should learn to control your own body in a way that is holy and honorable, not in passionate lust like the pagans, who do not know God" (1 Thess. 4:3–5, NIV).

There are many other passages in the scriptures that talk about sex, sexual immorality, and fornication: Colossians 3:5; Galatians 5:19; Romans 1:26–27; Jude 7; 1 Corinthians 6:18–20, 7:2; Acts 15:20; Exodus 22:19; Leviticus 18:22–23; Proverbs 7:1–27. The Bible very unambiguously forbids rape, incest, bestiality, pederasty, prostitution, homosexuality, and all other forms of sexual perversion, debauchery, and promiscuity. There are dozens of other scripture references I could list, but I think you get the point.

"Those who brazenly reject the authority of the Bible on issues of sexuality actually reject the authority of the Creator to determine what is right and wrong, natural and unnatural, allowed and forbidden. Ultimately, we must choose between biblical authority and sexual anarchy" (Dr. Albert Mohler).

So the biblical bottom line is this, sex is reserved only for marriage, period. Even there, it is only meant to be shared between just a husband and his wife. Sex between two unmarried people would, by definition, be considered fornication. Sex between two people who are not married to each other—where at least one of them is married to another—would be considered adultery. Both activities are biblically prohibited. Overwhelmingly, by today's society, these standards are considered archaic and outdated. In our culture of sexual revolution, abstinence before marriage is viewed as old-fashioned and unrealistic. Biblical morality is rapidly falling by the wayside and is being ignored, even within many of our churches, unfortunately. I'm here to tell you, though, that God's Word is eternal and never changes. Just because a majority of people don't follow it or may not believe in it does not change its truth. Just like you probably learned when you were a child, just because everyone else might be doing it, doesn't mean it's right.

Sex was never intended to be just a casual expression between any two people. It is a deeply intimate and spiritual (one flesh) experience designed to take place in a loving, committed, monogamous biblical marriage. Don't buy into the lies of today that sex is just a craving or desire to be satisfied and fulfilled like wanting to be warm, being thirsty, or hungry. Sex is not casual! God's sacred gift of sex to us is cheapened in today's "hook-up" culture, where bed hopping, multiple sexual partners, and "recreational" sex purely for pleasure devoid of any relational commitment is the norm. Don't settle for this cheap imitation that will never truly fulfill in the long run. It is so dangerous and can leave you broken emotionally and damaged in so many other ways—physically, spiritually, mentally, and financially.

I've heard the potential dangers of sexual immorality illustrated with two pieces of flypaper. I don't know if you have ever handled flypaper, but it is extremely sticky and very adhesive. If you take two pieces and stick them together, it is virtually impossible to pull them apart and to separate them without ripping and damaging both pieces. When you live a sexually immoral lifestyle and buy into the lie of casual or recreational sex, moving from partner to partner, you are opening yourself up to so many dangerous and damaging things. Just like those two pieces of flypaper, every time you have sex outside of its proper and intended context (marriage) you are joining yourself to that person. You are participating in the intimate, one flesh experience that is only meant for marriage. Then, every time that you move on to the next person, you leave a little bit of yourself behind. You are damaging yourself and that other person, whether you realize it or not. Flypaper that is continually stuck to things and then removed and stuck to something else over and over again will get damaged and eventually begin to lose its stickiness and potentially its ability to solidly adhere to anything at all. Eventually, if you continue down that dangerous path and keep joining yourself sexually to countless numbers of people, you potentially risk not only untold damage to you and others but also, possibly, the ability or desire to properly be able to adhere yourself in a right and committed God-approved relationship.

"Describing sex as 'casual' is like describing the ceiling of the Sistine Chapel as a 'nice little doodle.' That's what I can't stand— the people who diminish and cheapen sex are the ones who get to pass themselves off as 'sexually enlightened'" (Matt Walsh).

I recently had "the talk" with my two sons about the birds and the bees. I believe it is my responsibility as a Christian parent to teach and instill in my children biblical values, principles, and morals. Please allow me to make it abundantly clear, however, that I will never teach my kids to hate anyone who does not believe in or practice biblical morality. In fact, if you are one of those people, the Bible commands me to love you. My Bible doesn't say love your neighbor as yourself but only if they believe the same things that you do. We are all free to make our own decisions, and although I may not agree with one's lifestyle choices, I will not look down upon anyone because he or she sins differently than I currently do. I do not view myself as morally superior or better than anyone. I am just a sinner that has been saved by God's grace. On the flip side of that, however, I cannot and will not compromise on the authority of God's Word and its clear teaching on this issue.

To be completely honest, I have not always conformed to God's standards of morality myself. I did not save my virginity for my wife. I wish that I had. My wife was a virgin when we got married, and I thank God that she kept herself pure. I have been forgiven, but I deeply regret dishonoring my Lord and sinning against Him. All of us will have temptation cross our paths at times; I know I have. By God's grace, through His power and indwelling Holy Spirit, He gives me the strength to overcome and resist temptation. We are told to walk in the Spirit so that we will not fulfill the lust of the flesh. As a born-again child of God, you are not a slave to sin.

I just barely scratched the surface on this topic. I simply wanted to convey what the biblical position on sex is. Some people distort and twist the scriptures in a futile effort to try to update the Bible's morality standards. This is usually done in an effort to try and justify their own immoral lifestyle that they don't want to give up. God's Word, however, is clear, eternal, unchanging, and needs no updating. As has been said before, the Bible is not a bag of trail mix, you can't just pick out the pieces you like and ignore the rest.

I hope that this chapter may have encouraged you to dig deeper into God's Word to study this subject in-depth for yourself. If you are currently engaged in a sexually immoral relationship, it is never too late to turn to God and ask for His forgiveness. That is the beautiful thing about God and His grace, love, and mercy. Just because you may have crossed the line in this area does not mean that you should just continue doing it. God is always ready and willing with open arms to accept and forgive us when we turn to Him in faith and repentance, confessing our sins (1st John 1:9). I close this chapter with a poem that I wrote on this subject. As always, I pray that it will be an encouragement and a blessing to you.

A Biblical View of Sex

Its main purposes encompass so much more than
simply physical pleasure and procreation.
It's the fulfillment of God's created order in marriage;
don't settle for a counterfeit or cheap imitation.
There is a term for if you have sex and you are not
yet married; it's called fornication, not dating.
Because most people are doing it doesn't make it
right; if you are unwed, you should be waiting.
God created sex to be sacred between a husband and
wife, meant to be shared with only your spouse.
Prior to marriage, this gift is not to be enjoyed; you
shouldn't be living together and playing house.
It is a beautiful thing, but only meant to take place
within the confines of the marital institution.
This seems to be an entirely foreign concept that is
laughed at in our culture of sexual revolution.
Kept inside of its intended boundaries, it's a blessing
that brings warmth like the flames in a fireplace.
Out of its proper context, those same flames can burn
down your home with consequences you can't erase.
Any deviation at all from this biblical pattern violates
God's original and unchanging design.
It matters not that society deems it acceptable or the
description of marital union they redefine.
I urge you not to sacrifice your sexual purity on
the ungodly altar of burning lust and desire.
Your virginity can only be given away once, if lost,
it is not something that you can reacquire.
The sexually immoral person sins against their own
body when they ignore God's moral decrees.

There are dire ramifications to ignoring His commands
and instead doing whatever you please.
Using a condom does not make sex outside of
marriage safe or, for that matter, wise.
It's like saying that wearing a seatbelt makes
drunk driving safe; they are both lies.
So teach your kids the truth and biblical principles
as it relates to the birds and the bees,
The dangers and consequences of sin, giving in to
temptation, worldly wisdom, and STDs.
Don't buy into the ungodly values the media pushes
or Hollywood's films that are X-rated.
Sex is not to be a casual thing void of commitment,
and biblical morality is not outdated.

Randy Mlejnek

6

What Is Your Foundation Built Upon

It is hard to believe how your life or that of a loved one can change so dramatically almost in an instant. One day everything is normal for the most part and the next day your world can get turned upside down. A heart attack, a stroke, a car accident, a life altering diagnosis from your doctor, and everything can change on a dime. These events are not something that you plan for, and their impact can be devastating.

The gospel of Matthew chapter 7 supplies us with a contrasting narrative of two individuals. One of them built their house upon the sand and the other one upon the solid rock. When the storm came, the man whose house was built upon the sinking sand crumbled and was washed away. What you build your foundation on ultimately determines how you will weather the storm. The application is that you should build your life upon Jesus Christ, the solid rock. I think it is important to notice what I recently heard Pastor Matt Chandler highlight from this biblical passage. He points out that just because the wise man built his house upon the rock, it did not exempt him from the storm. Yes, only one house stood, but the same storm hit both houses.

The storms of life will come; they are inevitable. The question is, what have you built your foundation upon? In February of 2016, my family was given devastating news. We discovered that my mother-in-law Debbie had a large, malignant, high-grade, terminal brain tumor that covered a significant portion of her frontal lobe. It could not be surgically removed. This unexpected news shook our family to its core. Exactly two months later, at the age of fifty-eight, she lost her life to cancer. She was a shining example of someone who had built her life upon the solid rock of Christ Jesus. Even in the face of such adversity, she displayed great strength and an unwavering faith in God. One of her favorite songs and words that she lived by is "It Is Well with My Soul." She maintained a strength and calmness even when the rest of us were emotional train wrecks. Facing imminent death, she bravely expressed a desire to be strong for her grandchildren. She specifically mentioned being strong for my seven-year-old daughter Mary to show her that if she ever faces a trial such as hers, she does not need to be afraid. I love her, I admire her, and I hope that someday, I turn out to be half the Christian that she was.

When my wife posted the news regarding my mother-in-law on Facebook, the immediate response was overwhelming. So many people gave encouraging words, let us know they were praying, and offered any help or assistance that we might need. It is a testimony to how many lives Debbie had touched in a positive way. She wore so many hats. She was a daughter, a wife, a mother, a Grammy, a sister, a friend, and she would tell you, most important of all, she was a child of God. She lived a dedicated life in humble service to her Savior. She taught Sunday school classes, led Bible studies and devotionals, she counseled those who had been hurting and struggling in their personal walk with the Lord, and she opened her own home up to those in need many times. She helped mentor many young people on their spiritual journey. She learned sign language many years ago and used that talent to bring honor and glory to our Lord. She helped lead deaf ministries at church and proclaimed the Gospel with her hands as she interpreted many a sermon. She loved me unconditionally from the time I married her daughter back in 1999. She treated me just like one of her own children and forgave me for things more times than I deserved. She truly exemplified a Christlike love and taught me many things.

Despite her trial that eventually took her life, God graciously gave her His peace that passes all understanding. We didn't understand the situation, we didn't like it, but we learned from her example to trust God in it nonetheless. Even though she didn't know exactly when or how the outcome would play out, she kept her eyes fixed on Jesus, and she knew that, above all else, it was well with her soul. She put her faith into practice and showed us what it means to truly trust in and rely upon the Lord.

My mother-in-law, Debbie Mills, was such a godly and precious woman who is greatly missed and will never be forgotten. She was one of the main people who encouraged me to start writing. I took her advice, and she is a major reason why you are reading these very words today.

I close this chapter with a poem that I wrote for my mother-in-law regarding her situation after we found out the news of her medical condition. I pray that you may find encouragement in it if you are going through a struggle of your own.

It Is Well with Your Soul

When life catches you off guard and throws you a major curve ball,
Be anxious for nothing and pray as was written by the apostle Paul.
When the odds are against you and the
chances of victory seem razor thin,
Remember that worry is the opposite of
faith, and therefore, to you, it is sin.
When you are given the worst possible
news regarding your condition,
Remember that your God is omnipotent,
and He is the Great Physician.
If this devastating information has just rocked you to your core,
Bowed before His throne is where you need to fight this war.
You won't understand it all, and it is natural to ask why.
Trust in the Lord for the strength that only He can supply.
Rest in Him and His Word, and He can give you peace.
Know also that our prayers on your behalf will never cease.
Your strong faith encourages me despite
a situation that seems so grim.
Your example has shown us that no matter
what, you will trust in Him.
Your peace is a testimony to His loving grace.
It is evident that in your heart, He holds first place.
We were devastated when we found out the results of your MRI.
Our children looked us in the face and
said, "Is Grammy gonna die?"
Searching for words, we tried to be strong
and not let them see us cry.
We don't know, but if she does, it will
only be a temporary good-bye.
That is the hope you have when on Christ the solid rock you stand.

Through this trial, you are not alone
because He will hold your hand.
Don't try to carry this burden; it is not for you to bear.
Give it over to the Lord and take it to Him in prayer.
So in this raging storm, don't worry; He is still in control.
Child of God, remember that it is well with your soul.

Randy Mlejnek

7

Angels and the Spiritual Realm

I do not wear glasses or contacts, and my vision has been tested to be at or near 20/20. You may have to wear corrective lenses in order to bring your surroundings into focus. Whether you have excellent sight like that of an eagle or the eyes of a dead rock bass, there are things that our human vision just can't see. Even with all of the technological advances in our modern age, the strongest microscope or telescope cannot tear through our physical observable reality to make visible the spiritual. If we could peel back the curtain of the spiritual realm and peek into that dimension, we would see such amazing sights. Yes, I believe in the existence of angels. I am by no means an expert on this particular topic. I would like, however, to share just some interesting things that I have learned from my study of God's Word over the years.

I believe that as the Bible teaches, these created spirit beings are utilized at times to carry out God's perfect will. (Yes, they are created, by the way. Satan is not God's brother as some religions teach. God is the only eternally existent One.) There are fallen angels too, sometimes referred to as demons. The Bible tells us that when Lucifer fell from heaven, a large number of the angelic host fell with him Some Bible scholars would say that number is one-third of all the angels. (Isa. 14:12, Heb. 12:22, Rev. 12:4). There is a battle raging, spiritual warfare if you will, that is taking place perhaps in another dimension that is beyond the capacity of our human eyes to physically observe. The Bible does tell us that on occasion, angels have revealed themselves to humans in various forms. Hebrews 13:2 states that some have entertained angels unaware. Angels are not a specific gender as they are not human, but they are almost always referred to in the masculine sense in the scriptures.

There has been a constant proverbial battle that has been raging, almost since the beginning of time, between good and evil. Spoiler alert: I've read the back of the book, and the good guys win! I believe that angels are used by God to intervene on our behalf, at times, to accomplish His sovereign purposes. God uses them to perform miracles sometimes. Yes, I believe in miracles too. What the unbelieving skeptic would attribute to an amazing series of coincidences, I believe many times is God's sovereign hand miraculously at work.

There are very few angels named in the scriptures. You may be somewhat familiar with the big three: Michael, Gabriel, and Lucifer. Of course, there are many more angels than just those three but we are not given all their specific individual names, if the rest even have names? There is much conjecture and speculation surrounding angels and the spiritual realm in general. Much of what is portrayed on television and in the movies is not biblically accurate either. We have many preconceived notions by what we have seen on TV and read in books as to what angels look like, but there is much we don't know.

The Bible refers to Michael as an archangel, so some have naturally inferred that there seems to exist some type of an angelic hierarchy, class, or ranking structure. Contrary to popular belief, humans do not die and become angels. The Bible does not speak of halos either but these symbols have been used in art to depict angelic beings.

There are also different types of angels described in the scriptures that seem to have their own specific roles or functions. Cherubim and seraphim are two such types. Angels seem to possess great power, much more so than humans (2 Pet. 2:11). It took only one angel to kill 185,000 people in 2 Kings 19:35. One angel was sent to destroy the entire city of Jerusalem (1 Chron. 21:15), and only two angels were used to destroy Sodom and Gomorrah (Gen. 19). Angels are capable of miraculous feats. They are obviously, though, not as powerful as God, and they do not possess limitless knowledge as He does. Angels are intelligent beings (Matt. 8:29, 2 Cor. 11:3, 1 Pet. 1:12), but they are not omnipresent. The Bible does not give us a specific number as to how many angels exist but does tell us that their number is great (Dan. 7:10, Matt. 26:53, Heb. 12:22). Matthew 26:53 refers to at least twelve legions of angels. From what I've read, *legion* is an old Roman military term that usually refers to around six thousand. So twelve legions of angels would be at least 72,000.

It cannot be dogmatically proven from the scriptures that Christians are personally assigned a guardian angel to watch over them specifically. There is a passage in Matthew 18:10 that some will point to and draw that inference, but the Bible simply doesn't state anywhere that angels are specifically and permanently assigned to us. We do know, however, that angels are sent to individuals—at times—to protect, provide, guide, and minister to.

So some people would call me crazy because I actually believe this stuff. The Bible clearly teaches these things, and yes, I believe the Bible is true and that it is God's Word to us. I believe that there is much more to this world than what we can physically see with our eyes. There are many things that the Bible teaches us about this subject, but there are also many details that we don't know about angels and the spiritual realm in general. I hope that this short little chapter helped to stir your interest in this topic, to get you thinking, and I would encourage you to do some further in-depth study of your own. I close this chapter out with a poem that I wrote recently about angels.

Angels

There is a spiritual realm filled with invisible
creatures that our eyes cannot see.
As a child of God, I believe that, at times, He
has sent them to watch over me.
Countless numbers of them exist in perhaps another dimension—
Heavenly soldiers, always at the ready, and standing at attention.
Angels aren't Christians who have died and earned a set of wings,
And they don't just float around on a cloud plucking at harp strings.
Created beings, they carry out orders in
line with God's perfect will—
Powerful and mighty, capable of wondrous
works, but God is greater still.
At times, they reveal themselves, and some
have entertained angels unaware.
They're sent by God to intercede for us
because of believing persistent prayer.
One-third of them rebelled, and from heaven's
army they were dismissed—
Now serving the evil one and known as
demons, yet not one is an atheist.
The Bible says that even they believe and
tremble at the Almighty's hand,
One day to be defeated when against Christ
they make their final stand.
Not too much is known of them and their world that is unseen.
They engage in warfare, and on behalf of good, they intervene.
There is Michael who goes to battle—his job it seems is to fight—
And seraphim who have six wings and are able to take flight.
There is Gabriel an archangel, a messenger;
God's truth he proclaims.

And cherubim, who stood guard in Eden
with a sword made of flames.
They declare God's holiness as they fly around His very throne.
They are spirit beings and so are not made up of flesh and bone.
Some would say that I am crazy and that I believe in ghosts.
They would say that I need psychiatric help and to be diagnosed,
That I'm intellectually weak and lean on my beliefs as a crutch,
That I'm old fashioned and from the mainstream I'm out of touch.
But I believe God's Word is true and that there is an angelic host.
It matters not to me what they say or the
knowledge of which they boast.
I believe in miracles and spiritual things that
remain hidden from our view.
After death, their eyes will be opened as a
different lens they will see through.

Randy Mlejnek

8

The Cross of Christ

The crucifixion of Jesus Christ on a Roman cross around two millennia ago was the ultimate display of love in action that has ever taken place. That God would enter His own creation in the form of a man for the sole purpose of dying for us is an awesome wonder to consider. When you think of a judge in a courtroom, seated on the bench, you think of justice and judgment. God is a holy and righteous judge, and as such, He could not just overlook our sin and pardon us. The Bible says that without the shedding of blood, there is no remission of sins (Heb. 9:22). This was portrayed to us all through the biblical narrative of the Old Testament animal sacrificial system that God instituted. That system was a foreshadowing of the ultimate sacrifice that was to come in the Messiah, Jesus Christ.

If God just overlooked our unrighteousness, He would not be a righteous or just judge. He pronounced His judgment upon us because of our sin. Romans 6:23 tells us that "...the wages of sin is death..." The penalty must be paid; we owed a great debt. Our sin separated us from a holy God. Then, the amazing part of the story is that the righteous judge came down from the bench and laid down His very own life for the ones He had just condemned. He paid our penalty. No greater love has ever been shown in all of history. This righteous judge illustration to give perspective to what it is that

Christ did for us on the cross has been told many times and with several variations. I like how the author and Christian apologist, Josh McDowell puts it.

In his book, *More than a Carpenter*, Josh McDowell uses a very simple illustration to show just what God was doing for each of us at the cross of Christ. He wrote the following: "An incident took place several years ago in the state of California that illuminates what Jesus did on the cross… A young woman was picked up for speeding. She was ticketed and taken before the judge. The judge read off the citation and said, 'Guilty or not guilty?' The woman replied, 'Guilty.' The judge brought down the gavel and fined her $100 or ten days in jail. Then the most amazing thing took place. The judge stood up, took off his robe, walked down in front, took out his billfold, and paid the hundred dollar fine. One might ask, 'What's the explanation of this?' The judge was her father. He loved his daughter, yet he was a just judge. His daughter had broken the law, and he couldn't just say to her, 'Because I love you so much, I forgive you. You may leave.' If he had done that, he wouldn't have been a righteous judge… But he loved his daughter so much that he was willing to disrobe himself and come down in front of his bench and represent her as her father and pay the fine."

The majority of religious beliefs in existence today dictate that you must work your way toward whichever supposedly divine being that is worshipped in order to appease them. It takes great effort, sacrifice, obedience, penance, self-mutilation, and sometimes, even murder or death to bridge the gap between man and god. Some religions teach that you should die for your god. The premise is *do*. In Christianity, my God died for me. He bridged the gap for us. God came down to man; we don't have to try and work our way up to Him. In fact, the Bible teaches us that we cannot do that. It says that all of our righteous deeds are as filthy rags (Isa. 64:6). As the line from the great hymn states, "Jesus paid it all. All to Him I owe. Sin had left a crimson stain. He washed it white as snow." With Christianity, the premise is *done*! That is why Jesus said from the cross right before he died, "It is finished."

Without the cross of Calvary, we were doomed, dead men walking. Leonard Ravenhill said, "Jesus did not come to die to make bad men good. He came to die to make dead men live!" The Bible says that we were dead in our trespasses and sins (Eph. 2:1). I like how Dr. Chuck Missler puts it: "You and I are the beneficiaries of a love letter, that was written in blood on a wooden cross, erected in Judea about 2,000 years ago." Second Corinthians 5:21 states, "For he hath made him *to be* sin for us, who knew no sin; that we might be made the righteousness of God in him" (KJV). First Peter 2:24 states, "Who his own self bare our sins in his own body on the tree, that we, being dead to sins, should live unto righteousness: by whose stripes ye were healed" (KJV).

Jesus took upon Himself the sins of the world. Yet the very Son of God, in the midst of His agony and pain from those who were torturing and killing Him, cries out, "Father forgive them for they know not what they do" (Luke 23:34). Again, no greater love has ever been shown. C. S. Lewis said, "The Son of God became a man to enable men to become sons of God." I close this chapter with another poem that I wrote. This one is about the cross, and it is the first one that I wrote where I tried to make the poem into a specific shape. This is called shape or concrete poetry. It is also sometimes referred to as visual poetry. In this case, the shape is a cross.

Suspended on a cross between heaven and earth
He proved His love and how much you're worth
With His sacrifice your debt He would erase
You deserved that cross, He took your place
Jesus said, "It is finished." In Greek, tetelestai
We were bought with a price that He did supply
God's blood was spilled upon the ground
In Him alone can salvation be found
It wasn't the Roman soldiers or the nails that held Him on that tree
He could have called ten thousand angels to come and set Him free
It was His love for you and me so that heaven one day we could see
He was bruised for our iniquities and wounded for our transgressions
You'll find peace and happiness in Him, not in earthly possessions
He suffered, was beaten, and with His wounds we are healed
Accept Him as your Savior and you will be eternally sealed
He died, was buried, and was three days in the grave
He rose from the dead and from your sins He can save
Upon His death the temple veil was torn
It was finished and a new covenant was born
The cross of Christ was a victory, not a defeat
With His resurrection His plan was complete
Forgiveness is offered not an automatic guarantee.
You have to accept it, this is His sovereign decree
You can come to the Father if He draws you first
Drink of His living water and you will never thirst
By grace, through faith, repent and believe
Not of works can you boast that you did achieve
This is the gospel of Christ, the Bible's good news
Your soul hangs in the balance what will you choose

9

Is Church Attendance Optional for the Christian?

Have you ever heard someone make the statement that they are religious, but they don't attend church? Or that they're religious but they don't believe in the Bible or in organized religion? Excuses for not attending church are easy to come up with. People will tell you that they are simply too busy and don't have time. It's amazing how much time those same people can find to do the things that they want to do. The truth is that we find time for what is important to us. I've heard people say they don't go to church because there are too many hypocrites in the church. I've heard it said that not going to church because of hypocrites is like saying I don't go to the gym to work out because there are too many overweight people there. Another excuse I've heard people give for not attending church is that they like to worship God outside while they golf, go for a walk, or while hunting or fishing. They say that people that go to church try to put God in a box and think that He can only be worshipped inside of a church building.

So are these excuses valid? Will God accept these reasons? Is regular church attendance optional for the Christian? I would contend that it is not optional. In fact, the Bible references church attendance in Hebrews 10:25 as something you should *not* forsake. I agree that we should not try to put God in a box and that you can worship and interact with Him anywhere at any time. The scriptures do plainly teach, however, that being a regular committed attendee at a church with other believers is something we should be doing. Now, I understand that there are some people who physically cannot attend due to medical, health, or physical disability reasons. A medical shut-in could still listen to a sermon on the radio or television, and I believe God understands their situation. I'm talking about the otherwise healthy and physically capable people who could attend church but choose not to.

The church is not a physical building. The church is the body of believers (the people) who make up what the Bible refers to as the body of Christ, true born-again Christians. A group of believers can meet to have church outside, in a tent, at a camp meeting, in the woods, in a cave, etc. It does not have to be in a physical brick and mortar church building with a steeple on it. Now, the clear example of the New Testament Christians is that they regularly met with other believers locally where they lived to worship God, to preach His Word, to encourage each other, pray, baptize, give offerings, participate in the Lord's supper (communion), to serve, to exercise their spiritual gifts, and to bear one another's burdens. They organized and gathered together regularly. If you want to talk about organized religion, this was it. We should be following that example as well and not forsaking the assembling of ourselves together (Heb. 10:25).

This is the way God set up and designed the Christian life, to be lived out with and among other like-minded believers who regularly gather together in His name. He did not set things up for you to be a solo Christian, trying to do it all on your own. Yes, we need to rely and depend upon God daily for strength, guidance, and wisdom. He also wants us to stand united together as a single unit or body to help lift each other up along this journey. We all make up different parts of the same unified body. We all have different jobs or functions to perform to help that body to thrive and accomplish God's will. God has given every true Christian at least one spiritual gift, and those gifts are to be used to edify and lift up the body of Christ, the church. They were not given to you to be kept to yourself.

If I ever found the perfect church, I would not join it because, then, it wouldn't be perfect anymore. It is important to understand that there is no perfect church because there are no perfect people. Churches have had their problems since the very beginning; just read through the New Testament, and you will see that. So how should you weigh your decision as to which church to attend? You have to measure your prospective church choices by the teachings of God's Word. The Bible is the final authority on all matters for the Christian. Does the church that you attend or are considering attending, line up with what God's written word says? Are their beliefs and practices contrary to the plain teaching of scripture? If so, that should make your decision quite simple. I would do one thing if I attended a church that taught contrary to what the Bible teaches. I would leave!

In addition to that, I would suggest much prayer over the decision on which church you and your family should attend. Seek God's wisdom and guidance to lead you. Churches come in all shapes, sizes, and *flavors* if you will. Find the one where God leads you. As long as the one you choose or are considering is not violating any clear directives or principles of scripture in their teaching, beliefs, and practices, I think it comes down to prayer and personal preference.

And what does it even mean when someone says that they are a very "religious" person anyway? As I alluded to previously, many times you will hear someone say, "I'm a very religious person, but I don't go to church." Or "I'm religious, and I believe in God. But I don't believe in organized religion." Usually, it means that they believe in God or a god (little *g*) to the extent that it is convenient for them. You will also hear people say that they like to worship God in their own personal way. In other words, they say that they believe in God (and maybe even the Bible) but only to the extent that He doesn't interfere with their life, their decisions, or make any demands upon them that they don't agree with. I've seen people even take the position that they believe in God, but they don't believe in the Bible. Well, they don't believe in the God of the Bible then. They believe in a god (little *g*) that they invented—in other words, a false god or an idol. They believe in a god as they think he is or should be and that is to be approached on their terms. They believe in a god that fits into their personal world view and their personal perception of what he should be like and what he should accept. Talk about trying to put God in a box. The problem with that is mainly this—that god doesn't exist. The true and living creator God has revealed Himself to us in the Bible. That is our final authority on all things to do with Him. In the end, your personal opinions about God do not really matter; what the scriptures say is what matters.

If someone says that they believe in God but not in organized religion, ask them if they believe in Jesus. Because Jesus commissioned the apostles after His resurrection to go out and teach others about Him and to build His church. The Bible says that Jesus is the head of the church. Jesus died for the church. Jesus wanted a church. They were very organized and formed and founded many churches. They got very organized and sent out people on missionary journeys and founded other churches. The message of Jesus, the cross, and His resurrection spread like wildfire. Jesus was not against organization. Those that say they are opposed to organized religion usually make that statement simply as an excuse to not attend church. I think that people who make that statement have neither a problem with organization or religion. What they have a problem with is being told that they are and will be held accountable to a holy God for the things that they do. Ultimately, they are afraid of an encounter with a perfect and holy God.

If, by organized religion, they are referring to religious leaders, institutions, and churches who have legalistic, nonbiblical, man-made rules that they expect you to adhere to, who only want your money and to control you, then I am against that too. There are plenty of churches out there like that today. There was a religious establishment back in the days of Jesus who were much like that as well. Jesus stood in stark opposition to their teachings. He took a dozen men and started with them to build His church. There are plenty of good Bible-believing, biblically based churches in existence today, and God wants you to be a part of one. People use this catch-phrase all the time, what would Jesus do or WWJD? The best way to know what Jesus would do is to look at what He actually did. The Bible says that "as his custom was he went into the synagogue on the Sabbath day" (Luke 4:16). That was the church of that day or the local place of worship. Jesus went to church, and so should we.

I understand the excuse about not wanting to go rub shoulders at church with a bunch of fake, hypocritical people. Many of them are one way when you see them in church on Sunday morning, and then, they live a completely opposite existence during the rest of the week. We see way too often in the news, stories about a pastor or religious leader who gets caught up in some type of illegal or illicit activity. The pastor of the church that I grew up in for over twenty years admitted to embezzling hundreds of thousands of dollars from the church over a very long period of time. He ended up in prison. It's natural to want to throw your hands up in the air and quit when you find out that a man whom you trusted and known your whole life was secretly fleecing the flock while consistently preaching about giving tithes and offerings.

At the end of the day, am I really that different from my child-hood pastor? Are any of us? Let him who is without sin cast the first stone. There were large periods of time in my life where I was just "playing church." I would show up on Sunday morning with my

Christian facade on and then live how I wanted to live the rest of the week. There were plenty of times in my life where I just stopped going to church altogether. My hypocritical inconsistency throughout my life as it relates to my Christian beliefs and values has, I'm sure, turned more people off to church and Christianity than I realize. I will have to answer to God for that one day. My former pastor's sins were made very public in the news and in our community. How many of us have skeletons in our closet we would be embarrassed, ashamed, or even mortified about if they saw the light of day? I have made many horrible decisions in my life and in my marriage that I am ashamed of. I would not want my whole life broadcasted across a big screen for all to see. I am certainly not without sin and am in no position to cast a stone at anyone.

So here is the application: people are not perfect. People will fail you, they will let you down, and they will disappoint you—some of them greatly and some in ways that will cut you deeply. Don't put your faith in another human being; put your faith in the only one who is perfect, the Lord Jesus Christ. He will never fail you. He will never leave you or forsake you. There will never be a shortage of pastors or parishioners who will let you down or give a black eye, so to speak, to the cause of Christ. There will never be a perfect church in this life. We are all imperfect people, so find an imperfect church, go there, and do your best to do your part to do what God wants you to do. When others around you stumble and fall, when they mess up miserably, help them up, forgive them seventy times seven. (Matt. 18:22). Pray with and for them; allow Christ's love and light to shine forth from your life into theirs. And remember, they may be there to do the same thing for you someday. Don't let imperfect or hypocritical Christians cause your faith or faithfulness to waiver. Keep your eyes fixed on Jesus; look to Him, the author and finisher of our faith.

Attending church is a good place to go to hear the Word of God preached, to fellowship with other believers, to serve others, and to get your "spiritual batteries" recharged. You get around other believers, and you can sharpen each other spiritually. Although there will definitely be times where the church can help to meet your needs, I think putting extra emphasis on serving and trying to meet the needs of others is important. It is a part of the whole loving your neighbor as yourself principle that Jesus taught. The church does not simply exist to meet your needs. "The emphasis for us should be on contribution not consumption… So put away the shopping cart and pick up a shovel."[1] We should strive to be humble servant leaders as Jesus modeled for us. We should be actively involved and not just as the old saying goes "polishing the pine knot on the pew" while sitting on our butts.

God tells us to not forsake our church attendance. It is the way He designed and set up the Christian life to effectively function. I'm not saying if you occasionally miss or skip church services that you are out of the will of God. Life happens; you get sick or your work schedule might only allow you to attend every other Sunday (like mine does). If, however, you never attend or rarely attend, I would challenge you to do some self-examination in light of God's Word. It is important to take note that going to church does not save you or make you a Christian. It doesn't make you a Christian any more than going into a horse stall makes you a horse. We are saved by God's grace through faith in Christ alone (Eph. 2:8–9). Going to church is important and vital to your spiritual growth, but the church can't save your soul, only Jesus can. If you are truly a child of God, you cannot ever lose your salvation. So as a Christian, not going to church won't cause you to lose your salvation, just like attending won't earn it for you either.

So, can you worship God on a Sunday morning from your deer blind, the golf course, in your boat on the lake, or from the sidewalk on your morning jog? Yep, you sure can. Can you live the Christian life apart from attending church? You can try, but you will not be nearly as effective as if you were obedient to God's Word and His design for the Christian life. God's Word also says that if we are truly born again Christians, we will have a love for our brothers and sisters in Christ (1 John 3:14). If we truly love them, we will want to be around them. God's Word is clear as well as the example laid out for us in the New Testament—that He wants us to be an active part of a group of believers (a church) that regularly meets together in His name. We should endeavor to be diligent and obedient students of His Word. Obedience to His Word is the best way to demonstrate your faith.

Jesus said in John 14:15, "If you love me keep my commandments." In other words, if you love Him, do what He says. He died for you; He wants you to live for Him (Rom. 12:1). Part of living for Him is by being obedient to His calling to be a part of a Bible-believing church. I close this chapter out with a poem that I wrote about church. I pray that it may be a blessing to you.

Church

In the Christian faith, it is essential to your
growth and to help you to thrive.
The Bible doesn't merely suggest it. It's more
like a command; see Hebrews 10:25.
It is the New Testament example to belong to
a community of like-minded believers.
To be able to bear one another's burdens, you
need to be both givers and receivers.
The service that you miss might be the one that you really need.
Come and hear from the Lord, and your soul He will feed.
It affords you the opportunity to give tithes,
show love, encourage, and to serve.
Your attendance is your individual responsibility;
you are not "graded" on a curve.
Our spiritual gifts are not to be kept to ourselves while in isolation.
They are to be used to build up the church and for its edification.
We all make up different parts of the same body,
and our absence makes us incomplete.
We have to work unified together; the eyes need
the hands, and the legs need the feet.
Many sticks together in a group will burn hot and very bright.
When one falls away from the rest, it will grow dim like the night.
Ministering in the lives of others, you
can't pour from an empty cup.
Come and hear the word preached and
allow His Spirit to fill you up.
Then, you can truly serve and be broken
bread and poured out wine,
Allowing Him to lead you and through your life His love to shine.

You must be wise in your selection because
non just any church will do.
Make sure that they line up with God's
Word and what they say is true.
You can't just be spoon fed; Sunday shouldn't be
the only time you open up God's book.
You have to do some work too, and your daily time
alone with Him must never be forsook.
So don't be a bedside Baptist and only attend
when your nephew is in the play.
Forsake not the assembling of yourselves
together; this is the will of God to obey.
Don't be a C&E attendee, where you only
show up on Christmas and Easter Day.
It's vital to your walk, and time to come back
to the fold if you have gone astray

Randy Mlejnek

---

[1]   Quote pieced together from Aaron Loy in an article he wrote entitled
Five Really Bad Reasons to Leave Your Church (www.aarongloy.com).

10

What Is Christmas?

It is that time of year again; the holiday season is in full swing.

As I write this, we are in between Thanksgiving and Christmas, and the decorations, trees, wreaths, and lights are up. Malls across the country are busier than normal with holiday shoppers searching for a deal. Parents are taking their kids to see Santa Claus and employee Christmas parties are being held with regularity. Some of you are busy making and mailing out all your annual holiday cards with a list that seems to grow a little bigger each year. One of the most memorable Christmas cards I ever remember getting was from my brother Tony and his family. He, his wife, and two young daughters were in the picture on the front. Everyone was smiling except for their youngest daughter, who had the biggest frown on her red face with tears streaming down her cheeks. The caption said, "Merry Christmas and Bah-hum-bug!"

Many of you are trying to figure out what gift to give to that person that seems to already have everything. A handful of you will be regifting that lame present you got last year that has been sitting in your basement for the secret Santa exchange. Church attendance is way up the Sunday before. Several stations on the radio are playing nonstop Christmas music. Last minute details of large family gatherings are being planned out, and it is being decided who is going to bring which dish to pass. Red, green, and nativity scenes are everywhere. That loved one you have not seen in a long time is finally going to be home for Christmas.

My kids enjoy drinking eggnog (nonalcoholic) which they refer to as "Christmas milk." The popular classic holiday movies of days gone by are replaying on television almost daily. *A Christmas Story* with Ralphie and his Red Ryder BB gun come to mind. That red bucket and the Salvation Army volunteer are ringing that bell outside of the stores. Christmas tree lots are full of cars. It is definitely a busy time of year, and we all have our own familiar family traditions as well as food that we always eat during the Christmas season.

So that word *Christmas* keeps coming up over and over again. Have you ever learned where it really came from and what it represents? *Christmas* is a compound word originating in the term "Christ's Mass." It is derived from the Middle English *Cristemasse*, which is from Old English *Crīstesmæsse*, a phrase first recorded in 1038 followed by the word *Cristes-messe* in 1131 (Wikipedia). It is an annual celebration to remember the birth of Jesus. Jesus is the only person I know whom virtually the entire world pauses to celebrate and recognize His birthday. His power and presence are still felt to this day over two millennia later. There is a beautiful Christmas song that I recently listened to that is definitely worth checking out. It is "A Hallelujah Christmas" by Cloverton. This song very much encapsulates the true meaning of Christmas.

Many are unfortunately trying to remove the *Christ* from Christmas and insert their own word, phrase, or meaning. The true Christmas story, however, will never change. In fact, it is meant to actually change us. You can no more remove Christ from Christmas than you can hydrogen from water without it completely ceasing to be what it actually is. Just as the old cliché goes, Jesus really is the reason for the season. Nevertheless, some people refuse to allow Jesus to have anything to do with their December 25. What does Christmas mean to you?

If you are not a believer in Christ, I challenge you to do something. Get a copy of the Gospel of John, read it, and call out to the Almighty God in prayer. Ask Him that if He really is who He says He is, to reveal Himself to you. No, I don't mean reveal as in physically appear at the foot of your bed. I mean reveal in the sense of Him opening your eyes to the power and truth of His Word. I truly believe that if you earnestly seek Him and His truth, He will reveal Himself to you. It may not be right away, but through some situation, person, or circumstance, I believe that He will allow your eyes and heart to be opened. I close this chapter with a poem that I wrote just within the last few days. I hope that it is a blessing and encouragement to you, and if so, please feel free to pass it on to someone else.

What Is Christmas?

About two thousand years ago, a virgin girl gave birth
To a baby boy named Jesus, the creator of the earth.
He was born in a stable and laid safe in a manger.
Do you know this child, or to you is He a stranger?
Looking into the face of God, it must have been such a view,
Trying to comprehend that your baby actually created you.
The arrival of this child was certainly anything but routine.
This was the first Christmas, the original nativity scene.
Wise men came to see Him with myrrh, frankincense, and gold.
This is the reason we give gifts, the tradition has taken hold.
God humbled Himself, took on flesh, and entered His creation
Because of His love for all, in order to save us from damnation.
God became a man so that He was able to die.
To pay for our sin, His very life He would supply.
It was the greatest gift ever given, never to be outdone.
For God so loved the world that He gave His only Son.
He was born to die so that we could live,
A greater gift of love no one could give.
So just remember that is the true Christmas meaning—
God coming to this world and on our behalf intervening.
So when you gather with your family to do the things you do,
Take time to read the Christmas story found in Luke chapter 2.
This time of year, don't forget the real reason for the celebration.
It's not presents, Santa Claus, trees, or food; it is the incarnation.

Randy Mlejnek

I I

What Is Easter?

The resurrection of Jesus Christ is the single event that sets Christianity apart from all other beliefs. The leaders and founders of every other major religion lived, died, and their lifeless bodies remain dead. Jesus rose bodily from the grave and is still alive today. At Christmas time, we celebrate His birth. With Easter, we celebrate His resurrection from the dead. It is one of the best attested to and verifiable facts of ancient history. There was a man by the name of Simon Greenleaf (1783–1853) who was the dane professor of law at Harvard University. He wrote a book weighing the claims of the four Gospel books against the laws of legal evidence. I highly recommend his book titled *The Testimony of the Evangelists*. He was one of the brightest legal minds to ever live. He concluded in his aforementioned book "that the resurrection of Christ was one of the best supported events in history, according to the laws of legal evidence administered in courts of justice."[1]

A lawyer by the name of Frank Morison set out to explain away the resurrection of Jesus Christ. However, after examining the evidence, he was convinced that the resurrection was indeed a fact of history. He later wrote a book on the resurrection that I also recommend, titled *Who Moved the Stone*. There are three other books that I own and have read that I would strongly encourage you to read that deal with the resurrection of Jesus and His life. They are *More than a Carpenter* by Josh McDowell (highly recommend!) and Lee Strobel's *The Case for Easter* and *The Case for Christ.*

There have been many theories proposed to try and explain away the resurrection. They vary from Jesus didn't really die on the cross to His body was stolen by the disciples. The Roman government was a brutal regime. Executing people was something that they did quite often, and they knew how to get that job done. The excruciating torture of crucifixion was a guaranteed life crusher. The spear thrust into His side at the end was nothing more than overkill. Jesus was most certainly dead when they took Him off that cross. This is also one of the most well-documented facts of ancient history. There are both biblical and multiple nonbiblical sources that confirm this. The establishment of this fact is very important for the discussion at hand because you cannot have a resurrection without first having a death.

Jesus was put in that tomb lifeless. There was a massive stone rolled in place to cover the entrance. A Roman seal was placed on the tomb. There was also a Roman guard unit put in place to watch over things. The theory that the disciples stole the body of Jesus is a very weak argument considering the aforementioned facts. They had neither the means, motive, nor the opportunity to steal the body. The detractors of Jesus that wanted to stop His popularity, His movement, and His followers in their tracks would have only had to do one thing. All they would have had to do was show the lifeless body of Jesus to the crowds. The fact remains that they could not do that because He was alive, the stone was rolled away, and the tomb was empty! By the way, I've heard many a pastor say the stone was rolled away not to let Jesus out, but to allow others in. The resurrection totally validates the Christian belief as a whole.

Not only did Jesus overcome death, but He also showed Himself alive and well to hundreds of people after doing so. Acts 1:3 says that He presented Himself alive for forty days after His death by many infallible or convincing proofs. He walked, talked, ate with, and allowed others to touch Him. The disciples who had gone away in defeat following His death were suddenly reignited in their faith in Him. Not only that, but they were willing to die for the belief in His resurrection, and many of them did. Now, many people have died and have been willing to die for their faith, but they believed their faith was true. No one that I know of has died or been willing to die for their faith, knowing it was a lie. If anyone knew that Jesus didn't really rise from the dead, it would have been the disciples. These disciples were suddenly changed and became on fire in their faith and zeal, preaching the message of Jesus's resurrection. They did so in the face of death and extreme persecution with complete boldness. Only one thing can adequately explain this—that Jesus Christ actually did rise from the dead!

I cannot emphasize this enough—everything hinges on the resurrection! For if Jesus did not actually rise from the dead, then we are all lost and still dead in our trespasses and sins. Completely and utterly hopeless would be putting it mildly. If you could explain away and rule out the resurrection, all of Christianity would crumble. It is the central supporting pillar of all that we proclaim. This is the great hope and life-changing truth about Christianity. It is the bedrock belief that everything else hangs on. I also believe that is the reason why opponents of Christianity attack it so fervently. If they could explain away the resurrection, everything else, including the rest of the Bible implodes and is meaningless. "If Jesus rose from the dead, then you have to accept all that he said; if he didn't rise from the dead, then why worry about any of what he said? The issue on which everything hangs is not whether or not you like his teaching but whether or not he rose from the dead" (Timothy Keller, *The Reason for God: Belief in an Age of Skepticism*). He lives, and because He lives, I can face tomorrow. Many opponents also attack Jesus's deity.

Believing in the resurrection is not difficult to accept when you truly believe and understand who Jesus was. He was God incarnate, in the flesh—solid proof text that Jesus is God. (Acts 20:28). The very God that created life itself entered His own creation and became a man in order to demonstrate His love by dying for us. Once you believe and grasp the true identity of Jesus, His divinity, belief in the resurrection is a natural next step.

When the apostle Paul was writing a significant portion of the New Testament, he specifically referenced the bodily resurrection of Jesus. There were many people who were still alive at that time who were eyewitnesses to the risen Jesus. Paul includes this fact in his writing. This is very significant and a strong selling point for the truthful authenticity of Paul's letters. This is information you would only include if you were positive that these eyewitnesses, who were still alive, would confirm your story and that what you were saying was true. Paul was basically challenging people in that day to go ahead and fact check his narrative. He was in essence saying that if what I'm writing seems improbable or unbelievable to you, go ahead and ask the many living eyewitnesses that can confirm my account.

There are many convincing facts that support the historical resurrection of Jesus from the dead. I'll list just a few of them for you: The conversion of Saul of Tarsus, the reignited bold and unwavering faith of the apostles, the hundreds of eyewitnesses, the early written accounts of it, the explosive growth and rapid spread of Christianity following, and (of course) the empty tomb itself. Just a bit more detail on Saul, whose name was changed to Paul after his conversion, for those who may be unfamiliar with his story. Saul was one of the biggest opponents of the early Christian church. He brought such persecution against it. He was one of their biggest enemies. He literally sought out and murdered Christians. He violently slaughtered them because of their beliefs. He went from that to becoming one of Christianity's greatest champions. He wrote the majority of the New

Testament that we have today. He was arrested, beaten, tortured, and persecuted himself for his beliefs in Jesus Christ. He went to his death, proclaiming the Gospel of Jesus. There is only one adequate explanation for such a radical transformation from one dogmatic position on the spectrum to one just as dogmatic on the other end. That is a direct confrontation with the resurrected Jesus on the road to Damascus, just like the Bible tells us happened.

I always enjoy a good quote, and I would like to include several that I like that reference the resurrection. The following is a quote from Lord Darling, former Chief Justice of England, regarding the resurrection: "On that greatest point we are not merely asked to have faith. In its favour as living truth there exists such overwhelming evidence, positive and negative, factual and circumstantial, that no intelligent jury in the world could fail to bring in a verdict that the resurrection story is true."

"There is more evidence that Jesus rose from the dead than there is that Julius Caesar ever lived or that Alexander the Great died at the age of thirty-three" (Billy Graham).

"I know the resurrection is a fact, and Watergate proved it to me. How? Because twelve men testified they had seen Jesus raised from the dead, then they proclaimed that truth for forty years, never once denying it. Everyone was beaten, tortured, stoned and put in prison. They would not have endured that if it weren't true. Watergate embroiled twelve of the most powerful men in the world-and they couldn't keep a lie for three weeks. You're telling me twelve apostles could keep a lie for forty years? Absolutely impossible." (Charles Colson).

I just heard Pastor John MacArthur make this statement recently. he said, "The question is not what proves the resurrection, but what does the resurrection prove?" It proves that Jesus is who He claimed to be, that He actually is God, and that the Bible is true. Easter is really about the resurrection of Jesus Christ from the dead and His victory over death and the grave. There has been much debate as to the origin of the term *Easter*, whether it be of pagan or Christian beginnings. Some people prefer to use the phrase "Resurrection Sunday" when referring to the holiday because of this. One English translation of the Bible actually contains the word *Easter*, the King James Version in Acts 12:4. For an in-depth and detailed article on the origins of the word *Easter*, you can visit the following web address: https://answersingenesis.org/holidays/easter/is-the-name-easter-of-pagan-origin.

The commercially recognized symbol of Easter is certainly the Easter Bunny. I personally don't have an issue with family celebrations for the kids that include some of the secular commercialized traditions like Easter baskets, candy, Easter egg hunts, and decorating eggs. We have gotten our kids Easter baskets full of candy and participated in those things. I don't have any issues with taking your children to the mall to get their picture taken with the Easter bunny or Santa Claus. I don't personally have an issue with having a Christmas tree in your home. I have done those things with my own children. I made sure to teach my kids the true reason for the holiday celebrations. What I'm simply trying to do is to highlight the true meaning of Easter. Let's not lose sight of that. Now, if you hold to a personal conviction against those extraneous secular traditions and forms of celebration during these holidays, that is fine, and that is your decision.

I close this chapter out with a poem that I wrote entitled *What Is Easter?* Once again, my prayer is that you may find it a blessing and an encouragement.

What Is Easter?

The event sets Christianity apart from every other belief.
Of all the proofs that Jesus was God, this one is chief.
He conquered death; it is the most remarkable fact of history.
How anyone claims to deny it is to me a downright mystery.
For if Christ had not risen our faith would be in vain,
Still dead in our sins and salvation unable to obtain.
He died, was buried, then rose on the third day.
He is the door to heaven; there is no other way.
The women were told, why do you seek
the living here among the dead?
They ran to tell the disciples, and very
quickly, the word began to spread.
O Grave, where is thy victory? O Death, where is thy sting?
The stone, soldiers, and tomb could not stop the risen King.
That Sunday morning, the power of love displayed His might.
His bodily resurrection caused the disciple's faith to reignite.
At His death, His followers went away in defeat.
When He arose, they were bold, never to retreat.
He showed Himself alive to over five hundred on a single day,
And the fact that the tomb was empty just can't be explained away.
Thomas touched his nail prints and put his hand in His side.
His doubts were erased; his request for proof had been supplied.
He ascended and now sits at the Father's right hand.
One day to return for His own is what He has planned.
So Easter is not about bunnies, eggs, or
baskets of sugary confection.
It is about Jesus, His victory over death,
and His glorious resurrection.

Randy Mlejnek

Notes:

[1]   Quotation taken from Josh McDowell's book *More than a Carpenter*, p. 97 (Tyndale House Publishers, Inc. Wheaton, IL 1977).

12

When the Check Engine Light of Your Marriage Comes On

Do anything long enough and it will, at times, become routine. You can tend to go on autopilot and you may become comfortable. It is easy to lose focus and not put in the effort that you once did. You may think that things are going just as fine as they always have as complacency creeps in and begins to blind you to the reality of the situation. In actuality, things are slipping and being negatively influenced as problems start to arise before you even realize the damage that has taken place. This is true in so many areas of our lives. It happens to us in our jobs, our friendships, our personal walk with the Lord, our commitment to exercise and eat healthier, and of course, our marriage is no exception. It is so easy to take things for granted. Complacency is a slippery slope, and it is also the silent marriage killer.

Outside your personal relationship with God, there is no other relationship that should be more important than the one with your spouse. I'll be the first to admit that I am not the perfect husband, *far* from it. I am also certainly not a marriage expert. One thing that I have been pretty good at though is making mistakes. The way I see it, you can go through life basically one of two ways. You can learn from the mistakes of others who have gone before you, or you can ignore them and make those same mistakes for yourself. I think that the wiser and more prudent course of action would be to take those mistakes and try to learn from them so as not to repeat them.

If things are not going as well in your marital relationship as they once were, maybe it is time for some self-examination. It is like the saying says; when it comes to our mistakes, we are very good lawyers, but when it comes to the mistakes of others, we are very good judges. If what you are currently doing in your marriage is not getting the desired results but you keep doing the same things, it is time to re-evaluate. The old definition of insanity fits in nicely here, doing the same thing over and over again and yet expecting different results. Friction and difficulty in a marriage is unavoidable. Arguments, disagreements, troubles, and trials will happen. Newsflash: you both married an imperfect person. We are all selfish and sinful by nature, and eventually, those flaws in us will surface in the close quarters of a marital relationship.

A good marriage takes effort and routine *maintenance*. Compare it to an automobile for a moment. This comparison has been used many times before. And for those of you who know me well, I already know what you are thinking, but just bear with me. (I know almost nothing about cars, and I am not mechanically inclined whatsoever. I can't even tell you the last time I checked the fluid in my car's turn signal air bladder valve.) Let me try to articulate this analogy in my own words. If all you do is drive your vehicle around and use it for the things that you need without ever paying attention to the things that it needs, eventually, issues will arise. To operate at peak performance, there are certain things that need your regular attention. A vehicle needs the proper air pressure in the tires to go down the road smoothly. It needs the oil changed regularly as well as topping off the essential fluids. The brakes need to be serviced at regular intervals to avoid danger, and every so often, it needs a tune-up. You also need to pay attention to the warning signs and those little orange, red, and yellow lights that illuminate in your dash do actually mean something. If you neglect these things, eventually, problems will occur and they can be costly and potentially ruin your vehicle altogether.

As a society, we have been conditioned to think that this is not that big of a deal because we can always just trade it in for a new one. Unfortunately, marriages today many times end up the same way. If it is not going the way that you want it to or you are not getting what you feel you need out of it, you just go find another one. For the Christian marriage, divorce should be the very last option, not the first (or not an option at all). Don't misunderstand me; I am not advocating that someone should stay in a physically abusive relationship or be a doormat and turn a blind eye to an unfaithful spouse. What I am trying to say is that marriages today are taken too lightly, and people give up too quickly.

I've heard it said that the main goal and purpose of the Christian marriage is not so much happiness as it is holiness. If you are both committed to Christ and walking according to the guidelines as put forth in His word in your personal lives, it will make a difference in your relationship with each other. The times in my marriage where Amanda and I were doing what we needed to be doing in our personal walk with God and were right with Him have always been the best times. Don't let me mislead you; that doesn't mean that we did not have problems during those times. We just knew who to take them to, and we were allowing the Holy Spirit to guide us. You can't be right with God while holding onto unforgiveness in your heart toward your spouse. Being right with God and walking in a daily biblically committed relationship with Him will yield amazing results in your marriage.

Every vehicle also comes with an owner's manual. Many people don't even bother to look at it, and that can prove to be a grave mistake as well. If your car is meant to run on unleaded gasoline and you fill the tank with diesel fuel, you probably won't make it to your kid's soccer game on time. It is also important to know that even if you try to do everything like you are supposed to, you may still experience an unexpected breakdown or mechanical issue. If you do, you need to take it to the right place for repair. If your alternator goes out, you don't take your vehicle to the carwash. Many times, this is what we try to do in our marriages, isn't it? If you are having a communication issue in your marriage and you haven't had a real conversation in over a month, a box of chocolates is not what you need. Our marriage gets "sick" with a temperature of 103 with extreme dizziness and dehydration, and we try to just put a Band-Aid on it.

The Bible is your owner's manual for your life and for your marriage. You need to read it and follow it. Communication really is vital. For so many years in my marriage, the way that I dealt with problems was by *not* dealing with them. I just simply chose to try and ignore them and not talk about them. I would be like a stone wall with my wife when she would try to talk about an issue that needed to be dealt with. Just a word of advice, all that does is make the problems worse.

I've seen many marriages start to wither and dry up on the vine. Complacency had set in and the couple was more or less just cohabitating under the same roof as roommates. Is your marriage stuck in a rut? Are you going through a rough patch? Have you allowed a root of bitterness or resentment to spring up within you? When is the last time you put some maintenance work into your marriage? When is the last time that you have prayed for your marriage together? Are you going to church regularly? Maybe it is time to seek some professional help from a good Christian marriage counsellor. Have you been going along with the "check spouse" light on but ignoring it? Maybe your situation is dire and needs immediate repair? Is your marriage on the verge of dying and on life support? Don't give up! With God, all things are possible. He is the great healer, and He can turn your brokenness into something beautiful. God rescued my marriage once from what seemed like an impossible place of no hope. It was due to my sinfulness and selfishness. If your marriage is at that point, where it needs a miracle to hold on, remember that our God is able. Is your personal relationship with the Lord where it needs to be? Is there unconfessed sin in your life? Start there, with yourself, open and honest before a holy God. I close this chapter with a poem that I wrote for those who are struggling in their marital relationship. I pray that it may help and encourage you.

Don't Give Up

Neither one of you is perfect, and difficult
struggles will come without a doubt.
I'll give you some thoughts on marital trouble
that I know a thing or two about.
Friction is inevitable, and your mountain
may seem impossible to climb.
Maybe your situation seems hopeless and,
like you, are on borrowed time.
If you feel like you can't go on, and the relationship has no chance.
There is One who can reignite your love
and rekindle your romance.
If heartache and loneliness are crushing you
and you're in the midst of a trial,
Think back to the day that you said "I do,"
and you walked down that aisle.
You promised to stick it out through better or worse.
Don't let your marriage die and drive off in a hearse.
You have been through so much and come too far to give up now.
Remember your commitment when you
spoke the words of your vow.
There is still hope, and Malachi says God hates divorce.
Reconciliation is always better than regret and remorse.
You can't be right with the heavenly Father if
you are not right with your spouse.
It will take hard work and humility, and you
shouldn't throw stones in a glass house.
In other words, don't be critical of the other
but examine yourself alone.
Don't point out the speck in their eye when
you have a log in your own.

Let me encourage you not to give up, and please don't quit.
Don't throw your hands in the air, walk away, separate, or split.
If happiness and forgiveness seem like an impossible goal to chase
And you've lost your will to go on, let me introduce you to grace.
It is amazing and comes from God—if you'll only seek His face.
For you see, it saved my marriage once from a dark and lonely place.
I've experienced His miracles, and I can
tell you that they are very real.
You can't fix this on your own; give it over
to God, and allow Him to heal.

Randy Mlejnek

13

God Can Still Use You

Have you ever strayed off the path with your relationship with the Lord? I don't mean, did you get so busy this week that you didn't get a chance to read your Bible and pray on Tuesday and you skipped your Sunday school class because you slept in? I mean, have you ever really gotten off track, backslid, ran from God, stopped going to church, got caught up in addictive sinful habits or behaviors, destroyed your Christian testimony, and really messed up in a big way? I have—and more than once—I sadly have to admit. I can honestly tell you that I was miserable much of that time too. Deep down inside, I knew what I was doing was wrong. I felt terrible guilt and shame, yet I continued on for some time. I fought against it, tried to suppress it, tried to drown it out, ran from it. I was miserable because I was under the conviction of the Holy Spirit. I allowed myself to drift way off course, and I knew better.

If you are truly a born-again Christian, one of the most miserable places to be in this entire world is out of fellowship with God with unconfessed sin in your life. As I've mentioned before, there were times in my life where I was running from the Lord. Those "running shoes" may feel comfortable at first and for a time, but they will very quickly begin to cause you pain and heartache. Yes, there is pleasure in sin, but the Bible says only for a season (Heb. 11:25).

Never trade temporary pleasure for permanent regret. Ultimately, sin will not satisfy! It will leave you in brokenness and despair, and it can cause severe hurt and damage to those that truly love you. There are two different ways that you can go through life. You can learn from the mistakes and failures of others and heed their warnings, or you can go down those same roads that they did and suffer the same results. I'm here to tell you that it is not worth it. Fix your eyes upon Jesus, the author and finisher of our faith, and do not get off the path that He has set before you.

I am thankful for a God who pursued me, even while I was running from Him. He picked me up and set me on a new path. It's not easy to try and live down those sinful choices, especially to those who know you well. Many struggles will come your way, and many temptations will cross your path. Memories of a sinful past can haunt you if you allow them to. Our God is greater than our struggles. Your past mistakes do not have to define you. God *can* still use you! You can move beyond it, and you can get through it. He can make all things new once again. I heard a preacher say, God can take your mess and turn it into a message.

I don't know exactly where you are in your walk with God at the moment. Maybe you have recently come back into fellowship with God, and you are endeavoring to try and live for Him once again? You started reading your Bible, and you are attending church. But you feel that God could never really use you because of your past. Well, I'm here to tell you that He can! No matter what you have done, how far you have strayed, how many bridges you may have burned, God can and will forgive you (1 John 1:9), and He can still use you for His honor, His glory, and the furtherance of His kingdom.

No doubt you have read the following list of biblical characters and their infamous sins, shortcomings, or excuses on the internet or social media somewhere before. I want to put them before your eyes to help drive the point home that God can still use you. Noah got drunk, Moses was a murderer and had a stuttering problem, Jacob was a cheater, David had an affair, Jonah ran from God, Naomi was a widow, Miriam was a gossip, Martha was a worrier, Thomas was a doubter, Gideon was insecure, Elijah was moody, Rahab was a prostitute, Job went bankrupt, Peter denied Christ, the Samaritan woman was divorced—more than once, Paul murdered Christians, and Lazarus was dead! Yet look how greatly God used these people. If you are willing to confess your sins, ask for His forgiveness, and submit to His will, His way, and His Lordship over your life, God can make all things new again.

We are commanded to present our bodies as a "living sacrifice" (Rom. 12:1) to God. We are told that if we want to be followers of Christ that we are to die to ourselves, to pick up our cross, and follow after Him. We should start each day by attending our own funeral—die to self; to our self-will, our pride, our sinful desires; to allow God to have complete control over all our lives. It is taking our hands off the steering wheel of our lives and, by faith, allowing God to take control. Without faith, it is impossible to please Him (Heb. 11:6). There is a popular song called "Jesus Take The Wheel" by Carrie Underwood that illustrates this point. We are not our own; we were bought with a price. God never said that it would be easy. He didn't promise that life would be all roses, rainbows, and sunshine for Christians. Committing your life 100 percent to Christ will not guarantee you a residence on Easy Street. Trials, storms, and difficulties are sure to come, but God said that He will supply all of your needs according to His riches in glory.

Only in a right and committed relationship with God can true peace be found. No matter where you may be on this journey of life, It is never too late to turn back to God. I have heard it said this way, if you are not as close to God as you used to be, guess who moved? Are you a Christian that is still trying to hold on to the steering wheel of your life? Are there areas that you need to surrender to His control? God doesn't just want weekend visits from His children when we go to church on Sunday; He wants complete control. If you have recently gotten back on track with your Christian walk and are in doubt as to whether or not God could really use you because of how messy your past is, let me just encourage you to trust and follow Him. Shake off the dust of your past and allow God to use you. Another song that I really like is called "Something Beautiful" by Steven Curtis Chapman, and it really goes along with the theme of this chapter. I encourage you to give it a listen.

Let me also say, that the guaranteed recipe for backsliding on God is to neglect your prayer life and time in God's Word. Your daily prayer life and devotional time alone with God is of paramount importance. You let that go, and it is just a matter of time before you are heading down a road that you don't want to go down. Trust me! It starts right there. You have heard the stories about how a pastor or prominent Christian person gets caught up in an affair or some type of gross immorality. People say that they slipped up and backslid. That is the fruit of their backsliding; they backslid months prior in their prayer life and devotional time with God. That is where every backslider starts. People usually don't just "fall into sin." They put on their rubber waders and they gradually go deeper and deeper and before they know it, they are drowning in it. Just like the old saying goes, sin will take you further than you want to go, cost you more than you want to pay, and it will keep you longer than you want to stay. The good news is that God can restore. He can fix your brokenness, clean you up, and set you on a new path with new desires.

Again, I'm not sure where you are right now. Maybe tragedy struck your life, and you got bitter and blamed God? Maybe you are like me, and you backslid on God? Maybe you messed up bad, and you are struggling with guilt? Are you dwelling on memories of a sinful past and can't seem to get your thought life under control? If you are away from God right now, won't you come home? If you have come back but haven't gotten active and involved like you should, won't you allow Him to use you again? Will you give it all over to Him today and allow Him to reign on the throne of your heart and life?

I close this chapter with a poem that I wrote earlier this month that I feel is fitting for the topic at hand. Remember, God can still use you!

He Can Restore

Bearing emotional scars and haunted by memories of your past,
Are you paralyzed by fear and feel like the darkness is so vast?
Have you made a complete mess of your life?
Is it filled with heartache, bitterness, and strife?
Did you pick the wrong path and just can't seem to get on track?
He's waiting with arms wide open; He wants you to come back.
Have you fallen outside of God's perfect will?
If you surrender to Him, He can use you still.
There is hope even in your current situation.
He can turn it into a cause for celebration.
He knew of the many paths, which ones you would take
Of the poor choices that would cause your heart to break.
He can put back together the broken pieces and make you whole.
Come as you are and allow Him to heal your heart and your soul.
So come, lay down your burdens at the Savior's feet.
His grace is sufficient, and all your needs He will meet.
He can make all things new in your life once again,
And He has already won the victory over your sin.
Don't keep going the wrong direction; you have a choice.
Take a deep breath, be still, and just listen for His voice.
It may seem impossible, but that's what God does best.
Put your faith and trust in Him, And He will do the rest.
He still has a perfect plan for you despite your mistakes.
Something beautiful out of brokenness is what He makes.

Randy Mlejnek

14

Biblical Baptism: Meaning, Methods, and Myths

It is one of the first steps of obedience that God would have you to take *after* accepting His free gift of salvation. Repent and be baptized was the call of the apostle Peter on the Day of Pentecost (Acts 2:38). There seems to be much confusion, controversy, and diversity of stances surrounding the biblical teaching of baptism today. Some teach that it is a necessary component to your salvation while others take the stand that it in no way contributes to it at all. Some churches and denominations practice infant baptism while others will not do so. Some simply pour or sprinkle you with water, while others only conduct baptism by immersion. There are those that teach you can be baptized prior to salvation and others that hold to baptism having to follow conversion. Some churches say it doesn't matter how you baptize and others don't even baptize at all.

With all these variations in the belief and practice of this biblical ordinance set forth by Jesus, it is easy to get confused. What is the meaning of baptism? What is the proper biblical method or mode of baptism? When should you get baptized? What are some of the unbiblical man-made myths surrounding baptism? I am going to try and very briefly address those questions. This short chapter will in no way be an exhaustive discussion on this issue that covers every question or angle on this topic. It is meant simply to be a quick overview of it to get you thinking and to encourage you to dive into a deep study of God's Word for yourself.

So, what saith the scriptures? That is the question that really needs to be asked because, ultimately, that is what truly matters above all else. Does your personal belief on this issue or the practice of the church that you attend line up with what the Bible teaches on baptism? Before I endeavor to delve into this subject, I would like to point out that I am not a pastor or a theologian. I do, however, believe that the Bible's teaching and example on this issue is relatively straight forward. There are many godly believers out there who take differing stances on this issue. You may agree or disagree with my assessment that follows. I would encourage you either way to search and study the scriptures for yourself and not just to take my word for it.

So, is baptism a biblical practice that we should participate in? Well, even the Lord Jesus Christ Himself was baptized (Matt. 3:13–17). He was baptized by John the Baptist in the Jordan River at the beginning of His public ministry. So why did He do this? It certainly was not to receive forgiveness of sin as Jesus was perfect and sinless. My understanding from the Bible and from things that I have read by men much wiser than I is that one of the reasons He did it was as an example of obedience to His followers. I think that it was also as a divine declaration of the authenticity of John the Baptist and the message that he preached. Also, notice that the baptism of Jesus took place by immersion. Jesus was lowered down under the water, not simply sprinkled. It was symbolic of His death, burial, and resurrection that was to come. I think that His example is relevant for us today. Getting baptized is most certainly something that the Lord commanded and is something that He asks for our obedience in.

Nowhere in Scripture will you find an example or instance of an infant or baby being baptized. You cannot support this practice biblically. I would put this in the category of a man-made concept or belief. It is a myth that this practice can be supported with the biblical text. When we read about someone being baptized in the Bible, it is also described in terms of going "down to the water" or a river, being baptized, and then "coming up out" of the water. There are no examples in the scriptures of baptism by sprinkling or pouring. If biblical baptism was to be performed via the method of sprinkling or pouring, why—in the examples that we have—are they seeking out a body of water and then going into it? In John 3:23, it says that John baptized near Salim because there was "much water there" (KJV). To me, this seems to serve as a clear example of the method or mode in which baptism should take place. Also, as it pertains to the method, we know that it is to be done in the name of the Father, the Son, and Holy Spirit (Matt. 28:19).

You should study the meaning of the English word *baptize* as it was rendered in the original Greek language of the New Testament. The Greek word *baptizo* that our English word *baptize* comes from means to dip, immerse, or submerge.

I believe the Bible teaches that baptism is largely symbolic for the new convert to identify with Christ in His death, burial, and resurrection. The clearest way to picture this is baptism by immersion. As one stands in the water vertically, with the surface of the water running horizontally, it intersects with your body and is a picture of the cross. This is symbolic of Christ's death. As you are lowered down into and under the water, it is a picture of Christ's burial. Then, as you are raised up out of the water, it identifies you with His resurrection from the dead. Romans 6:3–5 and Colossians 2:12 talk about being buried with Him in baptism and being raised to walk in newness of life. The symbolism of Christ's death, burial, and resurrection is lost in any other baptismal method other than that of immersion.

It is symbolic and pictures or represents things much like when you take The Lord's Supper or communion (which also does not save you by the way).

Baptism symbolizes the Gospel in that it shows a symbolic demonstration of the death, burial, and resurrection of Jesus Christ. It also symbolizes what has taken place in the life and heart of the believer that is being baptized who has new life in Christ. We are identifying with His death as Galatians 2:20 states, "I am crucified with Christ..." We are buried with Him in baptism (Rom. 6:4) as we are lowered under the water. And we are identifying with His resurrection as we are raised up out of the water to walk in newness of life free from the power of sin in our lives (2 Cor. 5:17). It is also symbolic of the hope that we, as Christians, have of a future bodily resurrection.

So that brings us to this question: is baptism necessary for your salvation? I believe that the clear teaching of the scriptures show that it is not. Ephesians 2:8–9 plainly states that we are saved by grace through faith... *not* of works lest anyone should be able to brag that they earned their own salvation. Baptism is an act, a work, a deed, something to do or to be performed. Remember the words of Titus 3:5: It is not by works of righteousness which we have done, but according to His mercy He saves us. Paul in 1 Corinthians 1:17 said, "For Christ did not send me to baptize, but to preach the gospel..." So he definitively drew a distinction between baptism and the salvation Gospel message.

Probably the most well-known example used from the scriptures to show that baptism is not necessary for salvation would be the dying thief on the cross next to Jesus (Luke 23:39–43). He confessed the guilt of his sin, and He was told by Jesus that he would be in paradise with Him. He certainly did not get down from the cross and go get baptized before he died. There are numerous other examples in the New Testament where people were saved apart from baptism

(Luke 18:13–14, Luke 7:37–50, Matt. 9:2). Now, I certainly believe that we should get baptized out of obedience to the Lord, but I also firmly believe that baptism is not a necessary requirement of salvation. It does not save but is a testimony that you have been saved.

The clear example of scripture as to the timing of baptism is always after the Word of God has been received and then believed. In the Bible, baptism always follows conversion and never precedes it. This is also why many people refer to it as "believer's baptism." It is an external sign of an inward change that has already taken place. It is a public profession of your faith in Jesus Christ. You are identifying with Him.

In Acts 8:36 and 37, we read this: "And as they went on their way, they came unto a certain water: and the eunuch said, See, here is water; what doth hinder me to be baptized? And Philip said, if thou *believest* with all thine heart, thou mayest…" Acts 8:12–13 says, "But *when they believed* Philip preaching the things concerning the kingdom of God, and the name of Jesus Christ, they were baptized, both men and women. Then Simon himself *believed* also: and when he was baptized, he continued with Philip, and wondered, beholding the miracles and signs which were done." Then, in Acts 2:41, it says, "Then they that *gladly received* his word were baptized…" (KJV, emphasis is mine). In Acts chapter 2, Peter preached to a very large crowd. The Bible tells us that about three thousand people got saved, and then, the first thing that Peter instructed them to do *after* was to get baptized.

You only need to get baptized once. If you were baptized as an infant or were baptized before you accepted Christ, technically all you did was get wet. It does not matter how pure your intentions or that of your parents might have been. I am not trying to offend or take away from any personally meaningful experience you may have had. I am simply trying to highlight the truths of God's Word in relation to baptism as I believe they teach. I would encourage you to search the scriptures, pray, and seek wise, godly counsel on this issue from biblically competent individuals. If you have accepted Jesus Christ as your Savior and have put your faith and trust in him but have never been baptized, I would encourage you to follow our Lord's command to get biblically baptized.

So to recap on the main points, I believe we can confidently ascertain several things from the examples given in scripture and its clear teaching on this issue. Baptism is the first step of obedience the Lord expects you to take after being saved or born again. Baptism does not save you or wash away your sins. In order to be done biblically, it should be performed by immersion. It should take place only after conversion. Infant baptism is not found in the Bible and cannot be supported scripturally. I hope that this has helped you in your understanding of the biblical teaching on baptism. I close this chapter with a short poem that I wrote about baptism. As always, I pray that it will be a blessing to you and that you will find it encouraging.

Baptism

It's an outward expression of your obedience and of a changed heart.
It has no redeeming qualities, and as to
your salvation, it plays no part.
It is an external sign of an internal grace,
Showing the world that a change has taken place.
It symbolizes Christ's death, burial, and victory over the grave.
It does not wash away your sin, and your soul it cannot save.
To be biblically done, it is to take place after your conversion
And in a particular method, specifically by that of immersion.
Baptism by water represents the baptism by
the Spirit of your lost and dying soul.
Buried in the likeness of His death, then raised
in new life, you are made whole.
Standing upright in the water is a picture of the cross.
Lowered under illustrates our death to sin by His loss.
Raised to walk in newness of life, free from the power of sin.
Through the power of the risen King, our new life we can begin.
Performed in the name of the Father, Son, and Spirit,
A profession of your faith to all who see and hear it.
For the Christian, it is a conviction and a belief on which we stand.
Our first step of obedience to do as our blessed Lord did command.

Randy Mlejnek

15

The Lord's Supper:
A Brief Overview

Some people refer to it as communion; others call it the Lord's Supper or the Lord's Table. The title and the particular way in which the practice is administered varies depending on one's religious affiliation. It is that practice that was instituted by Jesus when he walked this earth some two thousand years ago. That day, in the upper room with the disciples, the Savior gave an edible object lesson that was spread out on a dinner table—a visual illustration of what was soon to take place, an event that would be set in motion and kicked into high gear upon His betrayal by Judas Iscariot, an ordinance that He instructed us to follow on a regular basis and to do so in remembrance of Him.

It was symbolic in nature and contained two primary elements: bread and wine. The bread, as He explained, represents our Lord's body that was broken for us as He became the sacrifice for our sins on the cross. The wine represents His blood that was shed for us and the start of a new covenant. Under the old covenant, the blood of animals had to be shed over and over again for the sins of the people. The blood of bulls, goats, lambs, and other animals had to be spilled. The Passover lamb under the old covenant had to be a spotless lamb without blemish. This was a foreshadowing of the perfect, sinless lamb that was to come (the Messiah). With the new covenant, Jesus became the ultimate, one time, all-sufficient sacrifice for the sins of all men. That is why He is referred to as the Lamb of God that takes away the sins of the world. As Hebrews 9:22 says, without the shedding of blood, there is no remission of sins.

This famous last supper with the disciples has been portrayed in paintings and on the movie screen countless times since it took place. Probably one of the world's most famous paintings is that of Leonardo da Vinci's, titled *The Last Supper*, which portrays this historical event. It is no doubt a familiar moment in time to most everyone. This was not just another ordinary meal, however, shared by Jesus and His followers. It was an ordinance, instituted by the Lord Jesus, that He commanded His followers to partake in on a regular basis. It was to be done in remembrance of Him and the sacrifice that He made for us.

Some churches and religious denominations participate in communion every service; others do so once a month or even once a quarter. There is no biblical command as to the specific frequency with which communion should occur. Jesus simply said to "do this" and "*as often* as you eat this bread and drink this cup, do so in remembrance of me." We know that partaking in the Lord's Supper was done so on a regular basis among believers. The details of the Last Supper is recorded by all four of the Gospel writers and is also written about by the apostle Paul in the book of 1 Corinthians. The main section dealing with the Lord's Supper can be found in chapter 11 of 1 Corinthians, verses 23 through 29. Christ's sacrifice of his own broken body and shed blood for the forgiveness of our sins is what we remember when we celebrate the Lord's Supper. We celebrate it because Christ's death was not a defeat but was, in fact, an overwhelming victory. Through His death, burial, and resurrection, we can have redemption, eternal life, and the forgiveness of our sins.

Partaking in communion does not absolve you of your sins, nor does it impart any additional favor, merit, or saving grace to you. The scriptures are very clear that it is not by works of righteousness that we have done but according to His mercy that He saves us (Titus 3:5). Ephesians 2:8–9 tell us that we are saved by God's grace through faith and that not by anything we can do ourselves; it is the gift of God and not by our own works so that no one can boast or be able to brag.

The scriptures teach that Jesus was the perfect, sinless, spotless Lamb of God and that He only had to die once for the sins of the world (1 Pet. 3:18). His one-time sacrifice was sufficient. A sacrifice that needs to constantly be repeated would not be a perfect or a complete one. I believe that the plain reading and meaning of the biblical texts that relate to communion show that it is a symbolic act to be done—as Jesus taught in memory of Him and His sacrifice for us.

There is no specific formula given in scripture for exactly how the Lord's Supper is to be administered. At my church, silver-colored metal plates are passed down each row of pews. One plate contains little square crackers (the bread) not much bigger than the size of a dime. The other metal plate contains little clear plastic cups of grape juice, not much bigger than a thimble. Our pastor reads a relevant scripture passage to the congregation, usually from 1 Corinthians chapter 11. A prayer of thanks is given for which each particular element represents (Christ's body and blood) before it is consumed. We are given a short time of personal reflection to "examine ourselves" so as to be careful not to partake in the Lord's Table unworthily as is instructed in 1 Corinthians 11:28–29, where Paul says, "But let a man examine himself, and so let him eat of the bread and drink of the cup. For he who eats and drinks in an unworthy manner, eats and drinks judgment to himself, not discerning the Lord's body" (NKJV).

There is some minor speculation amongst biblical scholars as to what exactly constitutes partaking in the Lord's Supper in an unworthy manner. Surely, having unconfessed sin in our hearts prior to participation would constitute taking communion unworthily. Participating in the Lord's Table in an unworthy manner can bring judgment or damnation to us according to God's Word. It would be better to let the communion plates pass by you and not to participate in the Lord's Supper if you have something in your heart or life that needs to be made right before God. We can be sure that we should be approaching this ceremony seriously and with a respectful attitude. It should not be taken lightly or flippantly.

I do believe, however, that the few brief moments we are given just prior to taking communion should not be the only time that we examine ourselves with an honest introspection. I heard a pastor mention once that he knew of a family that for the entire week before the Lord's Supper would be celebrated at their church, they would keep an empty plastic communion cup on their dinner table at home. This was to remind them of the service that was to come and to examine themselves all week long with a prayerful attitude.

There are many other side discussions that can take place regarding this topic, several of which can be quite divisive. I simply do not have the time to get into all of them here. I do hope, however, that this brief overview of the Lord's Supper has helped you to better understand it and the intended biblical meaning behind it. There are plenty of more detailed articles out there written by those much wiser and competent than I for you to find if you do a little bit of research on your own. Please enjoy the following poem that I wrote to go with this chapter, and as always, I pray that it will be a blessing to you.

The Lord's Supper

Our Lord instituted it at the Last Supper with
the disciples in the upper room.
At this gathering, He explained the meaning
of the elements they would consume:
A symbolic representation of the final sacrifice that would soon be made,
Spread out on a supper table and shared just before He was betrayed.
The bread represents the body of the Lamb
of God that was broken for you.
The cup represents His blood and a transition
from the old covenant to the new.
We examine ourselves and search our hearts
in a time of personal reflection,
Done in accordance with God's Word, but
also it seems for our own protection.
For Paul said you can bring judgment on
yourself if you partake unworthily.
If unconfessed sin is in your life, you should
let those plates pass, if need be.
The practice is mentioned in the Gospels and
in 1 Corinthians 11, verses 23–29.
Read the Word for yourself and discover why
we eat the bread and drink the wine.
The ordinance is symbolic in nature and imparts no saving grace,
Pointing to the cross of Calvary where Jesus died in your place.
So as you take communion, remember the
sacrifice that was made to set you free.
As often as you do it, recall the words of Jesus:
"Do this in remembrance of me."

Randy Mlejnek

16

Dressed for Success: The Armor of God

The Bible makes clear to us that the Christian life is a battle. We engage in warfare against a very formidable enemy, but not one made up of flesh and blood. We are in a spiritual battle that we are unable to win in the power of our own strength. Ephesians 6:12 tells us this: "For we wrestle not against flesh and blood, but against principalities, against powers, against the rulers of the darkness of this world, against spiritual wickedness in high places" (KJV). We are told that Satan is the prince of the power of the air (Eph. 2:2). He is a master at deception and has an army of demons at his disposal. We, on our own, are no match for this adversary. As Christians, however, we are far from alone! 1st John 4:4 says that "…greater is he that is in you than he that is in the world." God the Holy Spirit lives inside of us. One of the keys to this entire battle is found in Ephesians 6:10, where we are told to be strong in the Lord and in the power of *His* might.

One of the key factors to victory and success in warfare and just about everything in life is preparation. Abraham Lincoln has often been attributed with saying that if you gave him six hours to chop down a tree, he would spend the first four sharpening the axe. We need to be prepared for the battle spiritually by dressing the part.

Ephesians 6:13 says, "Therefore take up the whole armor of God, that you may be able to withstand in the evil day, and having done all, to stand" (NKJV). The individual pieces that make up this armor are listed for us in Ephesians 6:10–17.

The apostle Paul, who wrote the book of Ephesians, uses detailed imagery to give us a vivid mental picture of this armor. It would be battle gear that would be very familiar to Paul, namely that of a first-century Roman soldier. It makes a very fitting analogy to the spiritual warfare that Christians engage in. He lists each physical piece of armor and then ties them to a spiritual application for the believer.

The list starts with the belt of truth. The typical Roman soldier wore a tunic. It was basically one large square-ish shaped cloth with holes cut out for the arms and head. It was draped over the body. The belt, typically made of heavy leather, held everything together and kept any loose material from the tunic from becoming a tripping hazard or hindrance to his movement. The belt cinched things up tight and everything would hang on the belt. The belt of truth is mentioned first and, I believe, for good reason. Without the belt, which symbolizes truth, everything else falls apart. One of the main tactics of our enemy is deception. The Bible says that the devil is the father of all lies (John 8:44). So we combat his lies and deception with a sure foundation in the belt of truth.

Next is the breastplate of righteousness. This was a sleeveless piece of armor that covered the core part of the torso. This was a critical component to the soldier's battle apparel as it covered all the vital organs. Without this protective piece of equipment, a blow to the chest could easily prove to be fatal. It was sort of like an ancient equivalent to our modern-day bulletproof vests. Without the breastplate, the soldier would not last long and would most likely be doomed without it covering him. There are two main scholarly views for how this specifically relates to the child of God, and both are essential to living a victorious Christian life. Some hold to the view that this righteousness is the practical, day-to-day obedience to God's Word on the part of the believer. This breastplate, which symbolizes righteousness, is also something that we would be doomed without being covered with. So other scholars view this as the righteousness of Christ that is imputed to us upon salvation. It is credited to our account and we are clothed or covered in the righteousness of Christ because of His sacrifice for us on the cross—without which, we would be damned to hell.

Next is the shoes of the Gospel of peace. A soldier in Paul's day travelled rough terrain. They walked many miles on foot. They did not have the luxury of all the nice smooth paved roads and sidewalks that we have today. There were jagged rocks and uneven ground to traverse. Without the readiness and preparation of a good pair of shoes, a soldier would not be very effective in the fight for long. If you have ever stepped on something sharp and cut your foot, it greatly impedes your mobility. Swollen and sore feet affect your balance, speed, endurance, and ability to fight effectively. We are told to have our feet shod with the preparation of the Gospel of peace. We are to be prepared and ready to take that Gospel message to a lost and dying world. It is a readiness to move for God and to stand firm on His message. If you get busy moving for the Lord, you are sure to encounter resistance from the enemy. If you are actively serving Christ and making an impact for the kingdom, rest assured that you will run into opposition and that the enemy will throw obstacles in your path. If your feet have not been prepared with the sure footing and foundation of the Gospel of peace, you will be sure to get tripped up, stumble, or fall. I've heard it said that if you never run into resistance from the devil, maybe it's because you are both traveling in the same direction.

The next piece is the shield of faith. The shield was an important instrument for the soldier in New Testament times. It provided a way to block and deflect enemy attack. It would stop enemy arrows, spears, or the thrust of a sword strike. A group of soldiers could stand firm and interlock their shields together to make an even stronger and larger barrier of protection.

We are told to take the shield of faith to be able to quench the fiery darts of the wicked one. Without faith, it is impossible to please God. When the attacks from the enemy come, we can stand strong in the object of our faith, Jesus Christ. We must have that faith to be able to withstand and deflect those attacks we are sure to face. Just like those soldiers who stood firm together with their shields overlapped, we can support each other as believers best in a community (church) where we work together to support each other. A unified body, who helps bear one another's burdens.

The helmet of salvation is next up on our list. The helmet's purpose is quite straight forward—to protect the head and the brain inside of it. Whether you are a soldier, an NFL player, or just riding a motorcycle, the helmet is a critical piece of personal protection equipment. For the Christian, we protect our mind with the security of God's gift of salvation. We can rest sure in His promises and the eternal security of knowing our final destination. Satan will try to attack the mind with doubt, worry, and discouragement. The helmet of salvation is essential to defeating his attacks. We are told to have the mind of Christ (1 Cor. 2:16), and we cannot accomplish that without the helmet of salvation.

We come now to the Sword of the Spirit. All the previous equipment was defensive in nature. The sword is not just a defensive tool, but our main offensive weapon. The typical sword carried by the Roman soldier was anywhere from six to eighteen inches in length. This was usually carried in some type of a sheath and hung on the belt. It was always with them and ready to be deployed for combat at a moment's notice. This shorter-styled sword required the soldier to be practiced and familiar with it to be most effective and skilled in its use. The Sword of the Spirit for the Christian is the Word of God. We need to be as familiar with it as we possibly can be to use it most effectively. This requires spending time in it, reading, studying, memorizing, and meditating upon it. The Bible is quick and powerful and sharper than any two-edged sword.

When Jesus was in the desert and was tempted by the devil, He responded with quoting scripture to him. We would do well to follow His example when we are faced with temptation. In order to quote it, you need to be intimately familiar with it. We are told to hide His word in our hearts that we might not sin against Him(Ps. 119:11). It needs to be in our hearts to be always with us and ready to use at any time.

Many people forget the first part of verse 18 in Ephesians chapter 6, when talking about the armor of God and spiritual warfare. This is one of the most critical items in our arsenal. The first two words in the King James Version say, "Praying always..." We are told elsewhere to pray without ceasing (1 Thess. 5:17). We must not forget to pray. It shouldn't be an afterthought either, but the first thing that we do. The effectual fervent prayer of a righteous man availeth much (James 5:16).

That completes the full armor of God. Are you fully dressed and prepared for the battle? I would like to close this chapter out with a poem that I wrote on the armor of God. I pray that it will be a blessing and an encouragement to you.

The Armor of God

We are in a real battle but not against flesh
and blood as our military faces,
But rather against rulers of darkness and
spiritual wickedness in high places.
Our enemy is a master deceiver who is also
invisible and, therefore, we cannot see.
We are to submit ourselves to God, resist the
adversary, and from us, he will flee.
The key to victory for the Christian is
preparation, to be ready for the fight.
We are instructed to be strong in the Lord
and in the power of His might.
We must be properly dressed spiritually
in order to assure our success.
Ephesians chapter 6 lists the very battle gear that we need to possess.
The imagery is of a Roman soldier and given
to us with a spiritual application.
We are told to put it on in order to survive,
and so it requires our participation.
We must have on the whole armor of God
so that we may be able to stand
Against the wiles of the devil and all the
schemes that he has planned.
It starts by standing firm with the belt of
truth buckled around our waist.
It holds everything together, exposing the
lies with which we are faced.
Next is the breastplate of righteousness to
protect the vital organs in our core.

It is essential to our survival, and we must put
it on if we intend to win the war.
We are told by Paul to have our feet shod with
the preparation of the Gospel of peace.
There is rough terrain and when moving for
God the enemies, obstacles will increase.
Above all, we are to take the shield of faith to
quench the fiery darts of the evil one.
The object of our faith is to be in Jesus Christ,
God the Father's only begotten Son.
To protect our mind and our head, we are
to take the helmet of salvation.
This hope gives us eternal security and
assurance of our final sanctification.
Finally, we are to take the Word of God,
known also as the sword of the Spirit.
This is most effectively used by those that know
it well, and the enemy will fear it.

Randy Mlejnek

17

Have You Thought through Your Worldview?

We all have them and many people are unaware of what theirs is or that they even possess one to begin with. Not all of them are equal, and some of them are neither logical nor coherent. Some of them just don't make sense at all. Others refuse to adopt a worldview whose implications allow for the supernatural or miracles. Others refuse to adopt a biblical worldview despite any evidence presented to them. If they accept God and the Bible, then they are admitting that they are ultimately responsible to a higher power for their conduct. Without that belief in God, they then feel justified in whatever immoral decisions and hedonistic sinful activity they wish to pursue. Most people do not openly and honestly think through all the implications of their own. Many are self-defeating and will fall into a heap upon deeper scrutiny and logical reasoning. Some are so lopsided and full of gaps that they have to blend and borrow from others to try to allow theirs to make sense.

I am talking about worldviews. Some of you may be familiar with that term. For those of you who are not, allow me to briefly explain what a worldview is. It is not a physical view of the world as if viewing the planet from outer space. It is, rather, a philosophical view of not just our world, but also of all reality. I think Dr. James N. Anderson sums it up quite well in his book, *What's Your Worldview?* He says, "*...A worldview is an all-encompassing perspective on everything that exists and matters to us. Your worldview represents your most fundamental beliefs and assumptions about the universe you inhabit. It reflects how you would answer all the big questions of human existence...*" (As a quick side note, don't confuse a worldview with religion. Everyone has a worldview, but not everyone has or adheres to a religion—at least not in the strict sense of the word.)

Those "big questions" include things like, is there a God? If there is a God, what is He like? The origin of our existence, the origin of the universe, morality, and what the purpose and meaning of our life is—if there is indeed a true purpose or meaning to it at all. It also seeks to answer questions pertaining to our destiny. Is there an after-life, and if so, then what? Whatever your particular worldview, that is the lens that you look through to answer or seek to answer all those questions. You can't live without one, and it has a far reaching impact on your life. It affects your values, morals, behavior, relationships, goals, how you raise your children, how you think and feel, and your overall outlook on life and eternity. Your particular worldview will also directly impact how you vote, view ethics, the causes you choose to get involved in, and your views on societal and cultural issues of a moral nature. An example would be your stance on abortion, same sex unions, and the criminal justice system.

So as you can probably already tell; your particular worldview is a pretty big deal. Yet, as I said before, most people don't give much thought to their own. There are many different worldviews out there, and it is possible for people to change what their particular worldview is. As an example, two well-known authors and Christian apologists, Josh McDowell and Lee Strobel, used to hold to an athe-istic worldview. They both switched to a biblical Christian world-view through a lengthy examination of the evidence. They thought through the logical and, sometimes, illogical implications of their atheistic worldview.

Many times, it all comes down to which worldview is most probable and logical when all the evidence is taken into consideration. Also, which one most adequately answers life's big questions logically and coherently while also corresponding to truth and reality? There are many different worldviews, and the purpose of this chapter is not to define or list them all. That would require too much time and space. I will, however, list some of the more common ones for you. Remember that even these general ones can be broken down into subcategorical worldviews as well. There is a Christian biblical worldview, theistic, deism, pantheism, polytheism, atheistic, panentheism, and finite godism just to get you started in case you wanted to look those up and do your own research. I'll be honest; I did not know the meaning of all of them myself before researching this topic.

I believe that there exists only one worldview that can adequately, logically, and coherently answer all of life's big questions and make sense of our visible reality. That worldview is the Christian biblical worldview, and it is the one that I hold to. I firmly believe, and am convinced, that it stands head and shoulders above the other views. It has stood up to the most scholarly and educated scrutiny since its inception. It is reasonable and absolutely the most logically probable when all of the evidence and details are examined openly and honestly. I would highly recommend a book, at this point, that I read not too long ago titled *I Don't Have Enough Faith to be an Atheist*. It is by Norman Geisler and Frank Turek.

To illustrate how competing worldviews can have their foundation crumble under scrutiny and sound reasoning, I would like to relay a story told by Ravi Zacharias. He is also a well-known author, Christian apologist, and highly sought-after speaker. He has, for numerous decades, travelled the globe and lectured to countless thousands of people. He very often gets invited to large college campuses and even the Ivy League schools. His format is often one of a question and answer forum. He answers a broad range of questions usually pertaining to Christianity, the Bible, philosophy, religions, morality, etc.

At one particular Q&A forum at the University of Nottingham, a student with an atheistic worldview stood up and asked Ravi a question. I'm partially paraphrasing the interaction, but it went something along the lines of this: "How can God exist when there is so much evil in the world?" Ravi, seeing that this student's question was self-defeating, gave a brilliant answer. He asked the man that if he believed in evil, aren't you then assuming that there is such a thing as good? The student answered yes. Ravi continued and said when you say that there is such a thing as good, aren't you assuming there is such a thing as a moral law on the basis of which to distinguish between good and evil? The student again said yes. Ravi then said if you assume a moral law, you must posit a moral law giver, but that's whom you are trying to disprove and not prove. Because if there is no moral law giver, there is no moral law. If there is no moral law, there is no good. If there is no good, there is no evil, so then, what is your question?

It is such an eye-opening interaction and illustrates my point that not all worldviews are equal. The student's question self-destructs and implodes. It is like sawing the very branch off of the tree that you are currently sitting on. So many times people do not fully think through the logical implications of their own worldview. They then have to borrow from a biblical worldview to fill in the gaps in their own in order for it to even begin to make sense. You see, an atheist can *say* that there is such a thing as good, evil, and a moral law, but in their worldview, it is impossible to justify it. They believe that there is no such thing as God and that we are all just the result of some random cosmic explosion billions of years ago. They believe that we are just star dust that is fizzing chemical reactions and we exist by sheer random chance. If we all came into existence by sheer random chance, then our life really has no true meaning or purpose. If we die and then that is it and if there is no God, what does it really matter how we live our lives? You see, the atheist cannot logically justify good, evil, or morality if we came into existence by evolving from some primordial soup.

Hopefully I have at least encouraged you to think through logically and critically to evaluate your worldview, regardless of which one you adhere to. I close this chapter with a poem that I wrote on this topic. I pray that it will be an encouragement and a blessing to you. Keep in mind that although worldviews and religion are similar things, they are not necessarily the same thing. All religions will, however, fit under the umbrella of one particular worldview or another, but not all worldviews are religious in nature. So because my worldview is tied to my religion (Christianity) in portions of my poem, it may seem as though I am using the two terms interchangeably. I wanted to draw the distinction.

What Is Your Worldview?

It's not what you observe while looking down at our
planet as if from a satellite image in outer space.
It's a philosophical view of all that exists with a line of
reasoning, logic, and evidence that you can trace.
Everyone has one; whether they realize it or not, they
are not all equal, and some don't make sense.
To be reasonable, it must be logically coherent and
correspond to truth to give it a valid defense.
Although one's worldview and religion are
not necessarily inextricably tied,
Both of mine are based completely on the
Bible, so it is my ultimate guide.
Some view all religions as a long train with each
one represented by a different boxcar.
They say we're all heading to the same destination;
it matters not where on the train you are.
All roads don't lead to heaven, if you want to come
to God the Father, Jesus is the only way
All religions are not basically the same with only minor
differences, like a Ford versus a Chevrolet.
Most all of them are fundamentally different at their
core and, at best, only superficially the same.
With so many religions, how do you know which one
actually possesses the truth as they all claim?
Christianity is the only one that provides logical
consistency unlike every other view.
It adequately explains reality when the answers to
life's biggest questions are what you pursue
Like the reason for our existence, origin, the
meaning of life, destiny, and morality.

The results of your beliefs have eternal
ramifications; this isn't a matter of triviality.
The facts of life are not just a mystery yet to be
discovered, and objective truth can be known.
Many have to borrow from a biblical worldview to
fill in the gaps and make sense of their own.
You see, all the different worldviews cannot be true
because truth by its very nature is exclusive.
Some are offended by the Bible, for it teaches
accountability. And they find its demands intrusive.
The resurrection of Jesus is what sets Christianity
apart, causing it to stand tall above the rest.
He proved to have power over death, how does
your religious leader stand up to this test?
There are many people that are sincere in what they
believe, but the road to hell is paved with sincerity.
You are free to put your faith in what you will, but
ultimately, the truth is not based upon popularity.
Some hold to a view because it doesn't interfere with
their lifestyle, so they stick to it like glue.
It doesn't hold them responsible to a supreme higher
power for the immoral things that they like to do.
Is yours a matter of convenience, does it correspond to
truth, and have you completely thought it through?
Please, I urge you to examine all the evidence honestly,
and I ask the question, what is your worldview?

Randy Mlejnek

18

Eternal Security

The Allstate Insurance Company has been around for a long time. Their logo features two open hands cupped together, palms up, and next to it says, "Allstate, You're in Good Hands." They obviously want to convey to their clients and prospective clients that if you have their insurance, you are secure and in good hands. The implication is that they have you covered, and you will have nothing to worry about. For the Christian believer in Jesus Christ, we are also told that we are in good hands. As a matter of fact, we are told that we are held in the hands of God Himself. In the Gospel of John 10:28–29, it states, *"And I give unto them eternal life; and they shall never perish, neither shall any man pluck them out of my hand. My Father, which gave them me, is greater than all; and no man is able to pluck them out of my Father's hand" (KJV).*

There are many things I can think of that would convey a sense of safety and security. For example, a padlock, a big thick solid steel gun safe, a bank vault, the presidential limousine known as "The Beast," or his bunker deep under the White House. All those things pale in comparison to the safety and security of being held by the hands of Almighty God, the eternal, and omnipotent creator. Notice that there are two sets of hands in the text. We are said to be held securely in the hands of Jesus, who is then held securely in the hands of God the Father. Together, they guarantee our eternal security. God's grip is strong and secure, and there is no person or thing that is able to snatch us from His hand!

The topic of this chapter is one that has been hotly debated by Bible-believing Christians for a very long time. There are good people on both sides of this issue. This has been a heated topic of discussion among biblical scholars and theologians for centuries. Nothing I say in this chapter is going to be ground breaking, nor will it permanently settle the debate. I hope only to briefly convey to you my personal conviction about the eternal security of the born-again believer in Jesus Christ. A conviction that I believe is firmly rooted in scripture and logic.

So the question is, once someone gets saved, born again, and becomes a Christian, can he or she ever cease to be a Christian after that point? More precisely, can a Christian lose their salvation? My answer to those questions is no, a truly born-again Christian cannot lose their salvation. Scripture is very clear that we cannot earn salvation. Likewise, there is no effort on our part that can ensure it is something that we can keep. I've heard it said this way, "If keeping the law does not make me a Christian, how can breaking the law make me a non-Christian?" It is the unmistakably clear testimony of scripture as a whole that by no deeds of the law shall any flesh be justified (Rom. 3:20, Gal. 2:16). It is also clear throughout the scripture that we cannot do anything to earn or merit our salvation. It is a free gift of God's grace through faith and not of our own works (Eph. 2:8–9). We can take no credit for it, and we will have no reason to be able to brag when we get to heaven.

If we could earn our own way to heaven, Christ would never have had to die on the cross. Likewise, if we could lose our salvation, He would have to go back to the cross and die for us again. If we could lose salvation, it would imply that the sacrifice of Christ at

Calvary was insufficient to cover and cleanse us of our sins, past, present, and future.

Another passage of scripture that really drives this point home is John 6:37–40, which says, *"All that the Father giveth me shall come to me; and him that cometh to me I will in no wise cast out (v. 37). For I came down from heaven, not to do mine own will, but the will of him that sent me (v. 38). And this is the Father's will which hath sent me, that of all which he hath given me I should lose nothing, but should raise it up again at the last day (v. 39). And this is the will of him that sent me, that everyone which seeth the Son, and believeth on him, may have everlasting life: and I will raise him up at the last day (v. 40)."* In light of that passage of scripture, to say that you can lose your salvation is to say that it is possible for the Son to fail to do the will of the Father.

It is very clear throughout the scriptures that we are not saved by any system of works. It is simply by the grace of God. It logically follows, in accordance with scripture, that there is no system of works that we can do to keep or maintain our salvation once it is freely given to us. If our good works did maintain our salvation and get us into heaven, we would have much to be able to boast about when we finally got there. That belief runs contrary to the clear teaching of so many biblical passages. If it took my effort to keep and maintain it, I can assure you that I would fail. It is not based upon my performance but upon His promise!

Now, people that don't believe in eternal security can point to isolated passages in parts of the Bible that raise questions. It must be remembered that in proper interpretation of any written document, context is king. Every text has a context. We cannot ignore the overwhelming evidence and testimony of the biblical text when viewed in its entirety that our salvation is by God's grace and is totally separate from our own works or effort. Yes, God calls us to be holy as He is holy. Yes, we are called to live righteously, to deny ungodliness and worldly lusts (Titus 2:12). That has to do with the ongoing process of sanctification, not in acquiring salvation.

Our salvation, our righteous standing before God, is a one-time instantaneous event, whereby God declares us righteous because of the sacrifice of Christ on the cross. We are once and for all justified. The righteousness of Christ is imputed to us. He who knew no sin became sin for us that we might become the righteousness of God in Him (2 Cor. 5:21). Sanctification then is a process, separate from our salvation, whereby God sets us apart and helps us to be holy.

Those that believe that you can lose your salvation will argue that the eternal security belief gives one a license to sin. I believe, as the Bible teaches, that a born again child of God is a new creation (2 Cor. 5:17). We are all fallen sinful creatures, and we will never be perfect in this life. We were born with a sin nature. Once saved, we are a new creation in Christ though. That does not mean, however, that we will not sin. We need to remember that not all Christians grow and mature at the same rate. I've heard it put this way, It is one thing for *sin to live in* the believer, but it is quite another for the believer *to live in sin.*

When you get saved, you become a born again child of God. You are a part of His family. The Bible says that He gives us the power to become the sons of God (John 1:12). That can never be undone, taken away, or reversed. I have three beautiful children. No matter what, they will always be my children. Now, they may misbehave from time to time, and I have to discipline and correct them. But they don't cease from being my children. Their behavior may cost them rewards and hinder them from having proper fellowship with me, but again, they are still my children. It is the same way with our relationship with God—once His child, always His child. We may misbehave, and God may have to correct us. We may forfeit rewards at the judgment seat because of that behavior, but we are still His child. Just as our physical birth cannot be undone, so our spiritual birth cannot be undone either. It is somewhat interesting to note that those that believe you can repeatedly be saved today and then lost tomorrow don't get baptized again after each subsequent salvation.

The very nature of eternal or everlasting life that God gives to us when we get saved, is just that, eternal. If you could lose your salvation, it would be temporary life. How could a Christian ever have true joy if they had to constantly be worried about losing their salvation and facing God's condemnation? Knowing that at any moment, they could slip up and sin and then pass into eternity lost in hell. That would be living in fear, and God's Word says that He has not given us a spirit of fear but of power and of love and of a sound mind (2 Tim. 1:7). You would have to be constantly worried if you had been good enough or if you had done enough. That is a works based salvation and runs completely contrary to the teachings of God's Word.

In Christianity, the word is not *do*; it is *done*. There is nothing I can do to garner favor with God. Even my good and righteous works are as a filthy rag (Isa. 64:6), the Bible says. There is nothing that I can do because it has all already been done at the cross. Every other religion is about man having to work or earn his way to God to earn his favor. In Christianity, God comes down to man and made a way where there was no other way. Jesus paid it all; there is nothing we can do. That is why Jesus said on the cross, "It is finished."

A man by the name of Dr. Bob Wilkin talks about those that hold to the belief that you can lose your salvation as holding to a "daisy theology." He says it is a belief that God's love for us is always a bit uncertain. These people do not know where they are in their standing with God when they are uncertain whether a sin they committed caused God to take away their eternal life or not. It is like the little girl who picks a daisy and, one by one, takes off the petals alternating saying with each one: "He loves me, he loves me not." For those who do not believe in eternal security, they have an unsure faith and just have to hope that at the end of their life they end up on the petal that says, "He loves me."

I praise the Lord that I don't have to be unsure of my eternal destination. It is not a hope-so faith that He has given to me but a know-for-sure, confident one. 1 John 5:13 says, "These things have I written unto you that believe on the name of the Son of God; that ye may *know* that ye have eternal life, and that ye may believe on the name of the Son of God." My salvation does not depend upon my performance but upon His promises, and God cannot lie! Romans 5:1 tells us that those that are justified by faith have peace with God through our Lord Jesus Christ. Romans 8:1 tells us that there is no condemnation to those that are in Christ Jesus. Philippians 1:6 tells us that He that began a good work in us will perform it until the day of Jesus Christ. Ephesians 4:30 says that we are sealed by the Holy Spirit until the day of redemption. One of my wife's favorite passages of Scripture and the bedrock of this discussion is Romans 8:38–39. It tells us that *nothing* can separate us from God's love. I know that my God loves me. I have a sin nature and I will falter and fail from time to time, but I am clothed in the righteousness of Christ Jesus and that is how the Father sees me. And I can never lose that!

I close this chapter with a poem that I wrote on eternal security. As always, I pray that it will be a blessing and an encouragement to you.

Eternal Security

Once saved, always saved. Salvation from the Lord can never be lost.
Once applied, the infinite grace of God is
not something you can exhaust.
Belief in eternal security is my firm conviction,
but it is not a license to sin.
For those in Christ are a new creation; they
have been changed from within.
Salvation that could be lost would be like a
continual game of Russian roulette.
Our sins are washed in His blood; Jesus paid
it all. We no longer owe that debt.
It's not based on my faithfulness but on His
promise; that's reason to rejoice.
As one of His sheep, you will follow the
Shepherd, and you will know His voice.
Safe and secure in the Father's grasp and no
man can pluck us from His hand.
He is sovereign, and as to our eternal security,
He is in complete command.
He was the perfect sacrifice who only had to die once for all our sin.
If salvation could be lost, then Jesus would
have to die all over again.
It is about God keeping us and is not something
that we can work to maintain.
If our efforts could produce righteousness,
then the cross of Calvary was in vain.
1 John says, these things have I written unto
you so that you can know for sure.
Biblical salvation is a rock-solid assurance,
once and for all, eternal, and secure.

We can't earn it; likewise, our effort doesn't
ensure it is something we can keep.
All those the Father gives the Son will not be
cast out, nor will He lose a single sheep.
Our blessed hope does not depend on us but
upon Him, and His power is the source.
We are the bride of Christ, and I can assure you
that God's not going to get a divorce—
Sealed until the day of redemption by the Holy
Spirit and nothing can take that away.
Jesus Christ saves us totally and completely, to
the uttermost, and not just halfway.
Romans chapter 8 verses 38–39 tell us that
nothing can separate us from His love.
Our eternal security is out of our control; it's
something that He is in charge of.
It is not temporary salvation; it's called
eternal and everlasting for a reason.
Once saved, your position in Christ doesn't
change like the time or the season.
His grace is a gift and all because of what
He has done, not what we can do.
If you could lose your salvation, then keeping
it somehow depended on you.

Randy Mlejnek

19

You Can't...

There are many different paths you can choose to take while along life's road you travel. God created us with free will and the ability to decide for ourselves how to live our lives. We can choose to accept Christ or reject Him. We can choose to live for God, or we can choose to live for ourselves or other selfish pursuits. We can choose to obey or disobey God's Word. We make decisions every day of our lives— some of them good and some of them not so good. We choose who we are friends with and with whom we spend our time. We choose to go to church or not. We choose what to do with our time, our talents, and our treasures (our money). We choose to live a moral or an immoral lifestyle. We are free to choose, but we are not free from the consequences of those choices.

You can go through life one of two ways, you can learn from the mistakes of others who have gone before you, or you can ignore their experiences and make those same mistakes for yourself. Unfortunately, for me, I chose the latter more times than I care to admit throughout my life. There are so many truths in God's Word that are just plain unavoidable. Truths that we often don't listen to nor heed their warnings and we end up learning them the hard way.

One of the other chapters in this book is about the hardest lesson that I ever had to learn. In a nutshell, it is that you can't find true peace, true joy, or lasting contentment in this life apart from a right relationship with Almighty God. The sad part for me is that deep down, I already knew that truth. I learned it at a young age by reading and studying the Bible. Yet I tried to get around God's Word, and I ended up learning the hard way that it is something you can't do.

I ended up living for myself and chasing after the things of this world only to solidify the truthfulness and wisdom of God's Word. God has left us a road map to follow, a spiritual GPS if you will, in His written revelation. The Bible is our spiritual GPS (God's Problem Solver). Psalm 119:105 says, "Thy word is a lamp unto my feet and a light unto my path" (KJV). Ignoring God's Word is like trying to walk around in the darkness of this world, not knowing where you are going. You need His Word to be that lamp unto your feet and to light your path. If you try to stumble around in the dark, you probably won't make it very far before you bump into something and get hurt. Without the light to see, you will inevitably step in those pot holes and pits along the way. If you continue along without the light of His word guiding you, it may even lead to you falling fatally off the edge of a very steep cliff.

We are all responsible for our actions and the truths revealed to us in scripture. There is just no way to get around that fact. You may choose to stumble through life in the darkness—either completely spiritually blind (unsaved) or as a born-again Christian who chooses to stray from His commands. You may happen to stumble through life in the dark and only twisting an ankle here and there while avoiding the big cliffs. But we will all, at some point, stand before God's judgment seat—the saved before the judgment seat of Christ (Bema Seat, 2 Cor. 5:10) and the unsaved before the great white throne judgment (Rev. 20:11–15).

We only get one chance at this life. "Wherewithal shall a young man cleanse his way? By taking heed thereto according to thy word" (Ps. 119:9). The choices that you make in this life carry eternal ramifications in the next. Oh, how I wish there was a rewind button or that I could go back and do things differently. How many times have you heard someone say, "If only I knew what I know now and could go back twenty years ago?" Unfortunately, there are some things that you just can't do. I close this chapter with a poem that I wrote recently. I pray that it would be instructive and helpful for you today.

You Can't

You can't mock God forever. Don't be
deceived; you will reap what you sow.
You can't plant immorality, lies, and greed,
and then expect blessings to grow.
You can't separate the consequences from your choices,
but with free will, you can do as you please.
You can't avoid being influenced by the wrong people,
so if you run with dogs, expect to get flees.
You can't live in disobedience with the devil
and expect God to cover the lease.
You can't ignore His Word, live only for
yourself, and expect to have true peace.
You can't fill the void in your soul with anything
but Him, or you'll always be discontent.
You can't get around the Bible, the eternal truths
of His Word; you just can't circumvent.
You can't hide from the eyes of the Lord and will
eventually stand before His judgment seat.
You can't deny and ignore Him forever because
one day, your maker you will finally meet.
You can't serve two masters; it's either God or
yourself. Only one of you can hold first place.
You can't have true happiness apart from a right
relationship with God, a reality you must face.
You can't expect to hear from God while your Bible
stays shut with its cover collecting dust.
You can't reach your full potential spiritually without
fellowship, so church attendance is a must.
You can't take your words back once they have been
spoken just like a bullet fired from a gun.

You can't undo the damage from gossip, and repairing
a broken reputation is easier said than done.
You can't get to heaven without going through the
Son; the cross and His sacrifice is the only way.
You can't be promised tomorrow, so don't gamble
with your soul; you may not have another day.
You can't impress God by the car you drove, how much
money you had, or the vacations you took.
You can't get through the pearly gates without His
blood and your name being written in His book.
You can't take any possessions with you; I've never
seen a U-Haul being pulled by a hearse.
You can't get a second chance at this life, you can't
press rewind, and you can't go in reverse.
You can't avoid the inevitable; your day will come
when you walk through death's door.
You can, however, be forgiven, and I urge you to
ask the question, "Who am I living for?"

Randy Mlejnek

20

Unforgiveness

"To forgive is to set a prisoner free and
discover that the prisoner was you."
—Lewis B. Smedes

Meagan Napier and her friend Lisa were tragically killed by a drunk
driver in May 2002. The driver's name was Eric Smallridge. He was
convicted and sentenced to twenty-two years in prison. Megan's
mother, Renee Napier, was devastated. She wanted to see something
good come out of the tragedy, however. She began traveling the
country and giving seminars in schools, colleges, and churches on the
dangers of drunk driving and the power of forgiveness as she told her
story to thousands. You see, Renee came to the point of being able to
forgive Eric. Through Renee's decision to forgive him and through
God's amazing grace, Eric's life was radically transformed. Eric said
that he came to know Christ and accept His offer of eternal salvation
because of Renee's willingness to forgive him. He was even allowed to
join Renee at some of her seminars while still an inmate in 2010. Still
wearing prison shackles, his presence, coupled with Renee's powerful
testimony captivated audiences all across this nation. This is such an
amazing story. In fact, a well-known Christian musician and writer
by the name of Matthew West wrote a song about Renee's story called

"Forgiveness." (Feel free to visit www.themeagannapierfoundation. com to read more about this miraculous story.)

Forgiveness is not something that is easy to do in some cases, especially when the person or persons who wronged you are unrepentant for their hurtful actions. For the Christian, forgiveness is not optional, but rather a biblical command. Mark 11:25–26 states, "And whenever you stand praying, if you have anything against anyone, forgive him, that your Father in heaven may also forgive you your trespasses. But if you do not forgive, neither will your Father in heaven forgive your trespasses." Also, in Ephesians 4:32, it says, "Be kind to one another, tenderhearted, forgiving one another, as God in Christ forgave you." We are to forgive others even when they are not sorry and even if we feel that they don't deserve it. There are some people that will never apologize for how they have hurt or offended you. They will go to their death never asking for your forgiveness.

There are many other passages of scripture that speak to and demonstrate the principle and necessity of forgiving others of their offenses against you. Unforgiveness, when held on to over time, becomes a deadly poison that will give birth to bitterness, anger, pride, resentment, and even hatred. These things can literally shackle your mind to your past and will consume you from the inside out like a deadly cancer. These things can lead to severe mental health as well as physical health issues. You actually give the offender more power over you than they could ever get otherwise. We can't control what other people do, but we can control how we respond to it. I've heard it said that someone can only drive you crazy if you give them the keys. Unforgiveness can lead to you placing yourself in an emotional prison. It will eventually negatively impact all your other relationships, not to mention impede your spiritual growth.

In today's society, forgiveness is viewed as a sign of weakness for the most part. Getting even, making the other person suffer for what they have done, retaliation, and settling the score is what is touted by this generation. We are told that we do not need to swallow our pride and that revenge is sweet. This line of thinking runs contrary to the clear teaching of the Bible, Christian love, and the words of Jesus.

There are many sayings and clichés that have been repeated over the years that have muddied the waters of what true biblical forgiveness actually is. Probably, the most popular one is to forgive and forget. In order to understand what true forgiveness is, one must understand what it is not. Forgiveness is not forgetting. We are human beings created with a brain that retains memories. Our minds are not a computer with a hard drive that can simply be wiped clean. Many times a Christian will repeat the "forgive and forget" slogan and then erroneously cite the passage in Isaiah 43:25 or Hebrews 8:12, where it says that God will remember our sins no more. They will tell you that God forgets and that is what forgiveness is all about. That is not what those passages are saying. God is omniscient (all knowing), and forgetting is not something that He is capable of doing. What the passages mean is that for the redeemed child of God, He no longer sees their sin but views them through the shed blood of Jesus and His righteousness. The righteousness of Jesus is imputed to us.

Forgiveness is not condoning the behavior that was perpetrated against us. You are not saying that what they did to you was ok to do. Through forgiveness you are saying that you will no longer hold it against them. Forgiveness is not trust and many people get these two confused. Forgiveness is an act of the will freely given to another in an instant when you decide to do so. Trust, on the other hand, is earned slowly over time. There are some people that you might forgive that should simply never be trusted again because the risk in doing so would be too great. Forgiveness is not necessarily reconciliation. We should strive, as the Bible teaches, to live peaceably with all men. This is not always possible, however. Forgiveness is done on the part of the one who was hurt. Asking for forgiveness and being repentant is done on the other person's part. Reconciliation takes the willingness and effort of both parties though. Someone who is stubbornly unrepentant for their deliberate and hurtful actions can be forgiven but reconciliation will not be possible. Some people are simply toxic to you, can't be trusted, and do not have your best interests at heart. Sometimes, it is better to avoid those people and to let go of that relationship. You can and should still forgive them, however.

There is a parable in the Bible commonly known as the unforgiving or unmerciful servant found in Matthew 18:21–35. Peter is talking with Jesus, and he asks the Lord how many times he should forgive someone who sins against him. Peter throws out a number and says, "Up to seven times?" Jesus responds by telling him not seven times but seventy times seven times, or 490 times. Some translations render the phrase as seventy-seven times. Jesus was not setting a hard limit on the amount of times we should forgive someone and that after that limit has been reached, then we simply do not forgive anymore. Rather, He was making an emphatic point that we should always be willing to forgive someone of their trespasses against us. Seventy times seven was like a figure of speech in that day that implied an infinite number or a number that could not be counted.

The parable goes on to describe a king who shows mercy and compassion on a servant that owed him a large sum of money (ten thousand talents or approximately fifteen years wages of labor). The king forgives him of this debt. The servant then later went to one of his fellow servants that owed him a debt that was a fraction of the one that was forgiven him. This fellow servant owed him one hundred denarii (a denarius was approximately a day's wages). He grabbed the fellow servant that owed him the money and began to choke him, demanding that he pay him back what was owed. The king who had originally forgiven this man of his much greater debt found out about it and was furious. The last few verses of the parable state, "Then the master called the servant in. 'You wicked servant,' he said, 'I canceled all that debt of yours because you begged me to (v. 32).

Shouldn't you have had mercy on your fellow servant just as I had on you? (v. 33)' In anger his master handed him over to the jailers to be tortured, until he should pay back all he owed (v. 34). This is how my heavenly Father will treat each of you unless you forgive your brother or sister from your heart" (v. 35)

One of the lessons of that parable is that one who has been forgiven much should be willing to do the same to others. Forgiveness should be without limits. We should be willing to forgive much and greatly because the Lord forgave us of much.

Most of us know of family members who haven't spoken to each other in years over something that was said or happened between the two of them. Maybe you are one of those people? You both refuse to give in and avoid one another at all costs. In some cases, so much time has passed that you may not even remember all of the details of the original offense. Maybe you are harboring severe bitterness, anger, unforgiveness, and resentment in your heart? Sometimes, these sad stories end up with brothers, sisters, moms, or dads going to their graves without reconciliation and with forgiveness never having been given. None of us are promised tomorrow, and life truly is so short. Don't let your pride, stubbornness, or bitterness destroy you, a family member, or friend. Don't end up with a heavy weight of guilt and regret that you can never do anything to change because it is too late. Maybe you have a brother or sister in Christ you need to forgive or even ask for their forgiveness for something that you did? We need to always be willing to forgive because much has been forgiven of us.

I close this chapter with a poem that I wrote on forgiveness. I pray that it would be an encouragement and a blessing to you.

Forgiveness

It runs contrary to our sinful nature and
takes a deliberate act of the will.
It's cancelling another's debt and says they
no longer have to foot the bill.
It's not bringing it up again but giving them
a clean slate and a fresh start.
Holding onto the hurt allows a root of
bitterness to take hold in your heart.
It's not forgive and forget because our
memories don't have an auto delete.
It's taking retaliation off the table and realizing
that revenge is bitter not sweet.
Forgiveness does not mean that there will be no more pain.
If the hurt was deep enough, emotional scars will still remain.
Forgiveness is given freely, but trust must
be earned in order to be rebuilt.
It is not condoning what they did but simply
releasing them from their guilt.
Our Lord did not mean 70 times 7 to be a limit
on forgiveness in a mathematical sense.
It is an emphatic point that we should always be
willing to forgive others of their offense.
That does not mean we are to be a doormat
and suffer at the hands of abuse.
We are to exercise wisdom, and some
relationships need to be cut loose.
We are to bless those that curse us, love our
enemies, and turn the other cheek.
Repaying evil with kindness means that we
are loving, not that we are weak.

UNFORGIVENESS

It is a command for the Christian, and if
we obey, we will get our reward.
We aren't to try to even the score as vengeance belongs to the Lord.
It's applying the lesson in the parable of the
unforgiving servant and the debt of 100 denarii.
It's granting it to those that might not deserve it
and even when they don't say, "I'm sorry."
Don't let stubbornness come between you and
a loved one by refusing to budge.
None of us are promised tomorrow, and life
is way too short to hold a grudge.
Jesus said from the cross, "Father forgive them
for they know not what they do."
He is our perfect example, so don't be unwilling
to say the words, "I forgive you."

Randy Mlejnek

21

Biblical Prophecy: God's Authenticating Agent of Truth

There are many convincing pieces of evidence to show that the Bible is a miraculous, truthful, and supernatural book. The harmony and continuity of it is just one of them. Just to briefly elaborate on that, the Bible is actually a compilation of sixty-six separate books that were written over a period of around 1,500 years. It was written by about forty different authors from all walks of life and covers dozens of controversial subjects (sin, death, salvation, morality, etc.). It is written in numerous different literary genres, including poetry, history, law, apocalyptic, wisdom, personal letters, and prophetic literature. It was written in three different languages: Greek, Hebrew, and Aramaic. Yet from beginning to end, you have one harmonious story with an interwoven narrative that flows seamlessly together. This aspect alone is mind boggling when you really dig into it and nothing short of a miracle. I've heard this statement many times, and it is so true: the New Testament is in the Old Testament concealed, and the Old Testament is in the New Testament revealed. All the aforementioned details considered, the Bible is still a single cohesive integrated message system, and that alone is miraculous.

"The great discovery is that the Bible is a message system: it's not simply 66 books penned by 40 authors over thousands of years, the Bible is an integrated whole which bears evidence of supernatural engineering in every detail" (Dr. Chuck Missler).

Many things mentioned in the Bible have been confirmed to be accurate and true through archeological discoveries. People, places, and things relating to historical figures and events have been discovered that line up perfectly with the biblical text. "In just the Old Testament alone, there are over 25,000 references to people and places that correspond with archeological finds."[1] The Bible has been shown over and over again to be historically, geographically, and scientifically accurate. These things have been documented in book after book, laid out in detail. There are also numerous references in nonbiblical sources that corroborate and confirm details in the Bible.

If you would like to examine some of these evidences and findings for yourself, I would recommend starting with Josh McDowell's book, *New Evidence that Demands a Verdict*. Some of the most learned and skeptical scholars have, for centuries, tried to disprove the Bible to no avail. It can't be done. There has never been any type of discovery, scientific, historical, archeological, or otherwise that has ever been shown to disprove or completely discredit the Bible.

Of course, any piece of ancient literature is only as trustworthy as it has been accurately transmitted, copied, and handed down through the ages. To answer the skeptics who seek this avenue to attack the trustworthiness of the Bible as we have it today, I would like to point out a few things. There is more manuscript evidence for the reliability of the Bible than any other writings of antiquity. There are literally thousands upon thousands of manuscripts that have been discovered and preserved down through the years that we have to compare. The amount of manuscript copies from the ancient world that we have for other writers doesn't even come close to the

Bible—writings from the likes of Plato, Socrates, and Aristotle, the historicity and accuracy of which are never even questioned in the college classroom today. The manuscript evidence in existence for all three of them put together is only a fraction of what we possess compared to the Bible.

In the words of the well-known Greek scholar, Daniel B. Wallace, it is "an embarrassment of riches" that we possess regarding the biblical manuscript evidence in existence today. There is more manuscript evidence for the reliability of the Bible than any ten pieces of ancient literature combined. The other important point to remember on this is that the manuscript evidence for the Bible dates back to within a couple dozen years after Christ walked the earth. Most of the closest manuscripts of extra biblical writers, at best, only come within hundreds of years after the time that they were alive. The discovery of the Dead Sea Scrolls in 1947 was also a major find that absolutely authenticated the accuracy and reliability of the scriptures.

As compelling as the aforementioned evidences are, there is one that I feel stands head and shoulders above the rest. Probably the best evidence that we have to show that the Bible is a truthful and supernatural book is that of fulfilled prophecy. The Bible contains verse after verse where it accurately records history written in advance—prophecies which are neither vague or ambiguous, but specific and detailed. When you really dig down and examine this, it is difficult to logically come to any other conclusion than that the Bible is of divine origin. It must come from beyond our space-and-time domain. Much of the prophetic writing in scripture was a foretelling of history before it ever happened. The purpose of this predictive prophecy was to authenticate the credibility of God and, ultimately, His Word. These were not just educated guesses or coincidences that happened to come true. Many of these prophecies were recorded hundreds of years before they ever took place. They were precise in their details and timing. They came to pass with exact precision in their details and fulfillment without even the slightest error.

Some prophecies, written hundreds of years in advance, even predicted the exact date of their fulfillment. The Bible contains these prophecies that can be confirmed through mathematics and known history. These mathematical prophesies can be shown to be true and completely accurate by simply crunching the numbers and doing the math. One of the most mathematically precise prophecies given in the Bible concerns Jesus and His triumphal entry riding on a donkey (the original Palm Sunday) into Jerusalem. It was given in Daniel 9:24–27 and Zechariah 9:9. Most Christians don't even realize that the exact date of Christ's triumphal entry was predicted and given several centuries in advance. This prophecy alone is astonishing when you examine its details.

Over three hundred specific prophecies were fulfilled in Jesus Christ alone. This goes beyond the mathematical possibility of coincidence and any human reasoning to conclude that it was anything other than miraculous divine foreknowledge. Many of these were very specific prophecies like the one in Zechariah 9:9 that foretold that Jesus would ride triumphantly into Jerusalem on a donkey. This is one of the main things that separates the Bible from any other religious book or historical writing.

Some skeptics have stated that Jesus knew of the prophecies written in the Bible and just lived His life in a way to intentionally fulfill them. This argument dies a quick death when you realize that so many of these prophecies would be completely out of the control of someone to intentionally fulfill. Like, for instance, it was prophesied where Jesus would be born (Bethlehem: Mic. 5:2) and how He would be born (of a virgin: Isa. 7:14), the time of His coming (Dan. 9:24–27), that he would be betrayed for thirty pieces of silver (Ps. 41:9, Zech. 11:12), and the manner in which He would die (Ps. 22, Isa. 53). An interesting point on this last prophecy concerning the manner of His death (crucifixion), recorded in Psalm 22, was written seven hundred years before crucifixion was even invented.

There are many other things that were prophesied that were beyond human control like him being mocked, beaten, and spit upon. His hands and feet would be pierced, not a bone of His would be broken, His exact lineage and family line that He would be a descendent of, and that John the Baptist would be his forerunner. Some of these things were written down seven hundred years or more before they took place.

Dr. Peter W. Stoner (former chairman of the Departments of Mathematics and Astronomy at Pasadena City College) was able to determine, using the modern mathematical science of probability, that the chance for Jesus to fulfill just eight of the prophecies recorded hundreds of years before His birth would be one in ten to the seventeenth power! That's a one with seventeen zeroes after it (100,000,000,000,000,000). Stoner details these findings for us in a book he wrote titled *Science Speaks*.

I'm not that great at mathematics myself, so the illustration that Stoner provided in his book really helped me grasp the magnitude of this. He said that if you took 10 to the 17th power (10^{17}) of silver dollars and laid them on the ground in Texas, it would cover the entire state to a depth of two feet. He said, then, to take just one of those silver dollars and mark it somehow and then completely mix up all the coins. Then take a person and blindfold them and let them start anywhere in the state and walk as far as they wanted to. Then, have them pick up just one silver dollar. He said the chance of them picking the only marked coin would be the same chance that the prophets in the Old Testament had of writing just eight prophecies in their day that would come to fruition in any one man to the present day. Yet those prophecies all came to pass with 100 percent complete accuracy in Jesus of Nazareth. Remember, that is just for fulfilling eight of the prophecies; Jesus fulfilled over three hundred of them! Coincidence is ruled out by the science of probability. There is no other logical explanation other than the Bible actually being divinely inspired by God Himself.

The entire book is about Jesus. From Genesis to Revelation, cover to cover, Jesus Christ is revealed. You can find Him all throughout the Old Testament, not just the new. He is in Genesis 3:15, what is commonly referred to as the Protoevangelium or the first Gospel. This verse is talking about the curse on mankind because of sin and the provision by God of a future Savior, Jesus.

Although I have focused mainly in this post on the Messianic prophecies about Jesus, there are many others. The Bible contains thousands of prophecies. Some of them are about the future and others have already been fulfilled. There are literally hundreds of biblical prophecies that have already been fulfilled, all with 100 percent accuracy, just as they were written in advance—many of which you can confirm and verify using a modern encyclopedia at the library. Many of these prophecies were written hundreds and some thousands of years prior to their fulfillment. Many Christians don't even realize the sheer amount of precise prophecies recorded in the Bible that can be verified by doing a little research on the Internet. Prophecies that have accurately predicted when certain things would take place. Things like the specific prediction and succession of several world empires (Daniel 2 and 7: Babylon, Medo-Persia, Greek, Rome), the military conquests of Alexander the Great and his demise (Dan. 8 and 11), the Babylonian captivity (Jer. 25:11, 29:10), to the destruction of the Phoenician city of Tyre (Ezek. 26). For the skeptic, don't take my word for it; do some of your own research. And I think you will be amazed at what you discover. Maybe a book that has demonstrably shown time after time to have predicted the future hundreds of years in advance with pin point accuracy is worth your attention and giving a closer look?

I believe, with every fiber of my being, that the Bible is the inspired, infallible, inerrant Word of Almighty God and that He has preserved it for us down through time. I believe that He has authenticated His message to us through various means, one of which is prophecy. I close this chapter with a poem that I wrote about prophecy. I pray that, as always, you will find my words encouraging and that they will magnify the Lord and point you to the Savior.

Prophecy

It is a built in feature to authenticate the
origin of its message as divine.
Only He knows the end from the beginning,
so prophecy was given as a sign.
History was told before it happened; human
knowledge just can't explain.
It is supernatural and comes from beyond
our space-and-time domain.
I'll give you a few examples, but there are
thousands more you can read through.
Jesus isn't just in the four Gospels; you can
find Him in the Old Testament too.
The first Gospel message states that the
head of the serpent He will bruise.
This protoevangelium speaks of Jesus, also
known as the King of the Jews.
His coming was foretold hundreds of years
before He arrived on the scene.
He is the Lamb of God, and through His
sacrifice, you can be made clean.
Over 300 prophecies were fulfilled in Him;
His identity they precisely define.
Every letter, word, and number was written
in the Bible by His perfect design,
That He would be born of a woman in
Bethlehem through a virgin birth.
He would be betrayed by a friend and what
the cost of that act was worth.
Those thirty pieces of silver would then
be used to buy a potter's field.

He would be called Immanuel, and by His
stripes, we would be healed.
That He would be from the seed of David and rejected by His own.
He would be despised and beaten yet not suffer a broken bone.
He would be a sacrifice for sin, and they
would pierce His hands and His feet.
That He would triumphantly enter Jerusalem,
riding a donkey down the street.
We were told of His lineage, the exact
branch and limb of His family tree
And the purpose as to why He would come
is laid out in Isaiah chapter 53.
This is all miraculous confirmation that the
Bible, the Word of God, is *true*.
This evidence should be more than enough
to convince the skeptic in you.

Randy Mlejnek

---

[1] Quote taken from Chip Ingram's book, *The Real Heaven*: Appendix
A, page 165.

22

Christianity's Most Absurd Belief?

The biblical doctrine of the rapture is at least somewhat familiar to even the non-Christian population of our day. It has been brought to light in our modern day by being the main plot of several movies which were based off of the popular *Left Behind* book series by authors Tim LaHaye and Jerry B. Jenkins. Two of the more notable movies would probably be the *Left Behind* movie starring Kirk Cameron from 2000 and the movie by the same title starring Nicolas Cage of 2014. I have not seen either of them, nor have I read any of the books. And so I cannot speak to their consistency with the Bible's teaching on the subject, which should always be our final authority.

For those of you who really don't know what the rapture is or what the Bible has to say about it, let me try to give you a brief synopsis. The doctrine of the rapture is spoken of directly and alluded to in many biblical passages. You can reference 1 Thessalonians 4:16–18, 1 Corinthians 15:20–23, and 1 Corinthians 15:51–52 for starters. Basically, the Bible tells us that there will be a supernatural mass rapture or taking away from the earth of all true Christians—God's true church, the "bride of Christ." This will occur in a moment, in the twinkling of an eye, the Bible says. The Lord Jesus will descend from heaven with a shout and every single true born again believer (alive and dead) in Christ will be caught up, changed, and given a new glorified and incorruptible body. We will be taken away into the clouds to meet the Lord in the air as He takes us off to our heavenly home—an event that defies human reasoning and logic, along with the laws of nature and gravity.

The breakneck speed at which this all takes place will strain your mind to even ponder. The Bible states that the rapture will occur "in a moment, in the twinkling of an eye." Think of how fast a blink of an eye is, and it is probably going to be much faster than that. Massive numbers of people, perhaps multiplied millions, that suddenly vanish off the face of the earth in the blink of an eye, while the rest of humanity is left behind to go on living their lives.

Think of the global ramifications of such an event just in the very moment that it happens. At any given moment, there are an estimated five thousand commercial airplanes in the skies over the United States alone. How many Christian passengers, or perhaps pilots, will suddenly be raptured away? How many countless millions of vehicles are on the roadways throughout the world at any given time? How many drivers will suddenly be snatched up into the air, leaving their moving vehicle to careen off the road? The possibilities and variables of scenarios that will take place at the moment of the rapture are endless and astonishing.

To really sit back and contemplate the details of this biblical teaching is mind bending to say the least. The belief in the rapture is considered by many non-Christians to be Christianity's most nonsensical belief. I don't purport to fully understand it nor can I completely explain it in relation to finite human logic. I know that the Word of God teaches it, and I am a Bible-believing, born-again Christian. So by faith, I believe it. Now the question some of you might be asking is, when does the rapture take place? The short answer is that no one but God knows exactly when the rapture will take place. Some people have tried to set dates that have since come and gone only to look foolish when they were wrong. No man knows the day or the hour, and the Bible does not give us a date.

Now what the Bible does teach us about the rapture in relation to its timing is that it is imminent, meaning that it can happen at any moment. This teaching is known as the imminent return of Christ. According to the Bible, there is nothing left that must take place on God's prophetic timetable preceding the rapture of the church. That does not mean that it is going to happen today or tomorrow, although it very well could. Now there are different scholarly views on which point along God's prophetic timeline that the rapture will take place. I do not have the time or space in this short chapter to detail them all for you, nor do I claim to be an expert in biblical eschatology (theology or study of the end times). There are really just three main views in reference to the timing of the rapture. I will just list them for you to do your own research. There are post-tribulationists, midtribulationists, and pretribulationists. I personally fall into the pretribulationist camp.

Now, one more thing I would like to address, as you may have heard, is the objection that there is no such thing as the rapture, since the word *rapture* doesn't even occur in the Bible. It is true that you will not find the English word *rapture* in the Bible. You also won't find the word *Trinity* in the Bible either, along with several other theological terms that we use. Even though these words do not appear in the biblical text, their concepts are clearly taught in the scriptures. Believe it or not, you won't even find the word *Bible* in the Bible. You can do your own internet research on the origin and meaning of the word *rapture*. In Chuck Missler's book, The Rapture, it says, "…The Latin word *rapiemur* is used in the Latin Vulgate to translate the Greek word *harpazo,* which means 'to be seized.' In the King James, this word is translated 'caught up' (2 Cor. 12:2–4, 1

Thess. 4:17, Rev. 12:5) or 'taken by force' (Matt. 11:12, John 6:15, Acts 23:10)."

So what does all of this mean? Why should you care, and how do you prepare for the rapture? It means that the Lord Jesus could be coming back at any moment to take His children home to be with Him. The obvious question would be, are you one of His children? I don't just mean, do you believe that God exists? Simply giving mental assent to God's existence is not enough. I don't mean, did you pray some prayer, have you been baptized, do you go to church, do you read the Bible, or are you a decent and moral person? Those are all good things, but they won't save your soul. I'm asking, have you ever truly been saved, born again, regenerated, repented and believed, put your faith and trust in the Lord Jesus Christ and His finished work on the cross and His shed blood as the payment for your sins? The Bible says that you are saved by grace through faith and that not of yourselves; it is the gift of God. Not of works, lest any man should boast (Eph. 2:8–9) That is the first step.

You should care about the rapture because if you are not saved, you will be—like the movies and the books say—left behind. Left behind to face the seven year tribulation and devastation that will come upon the earth. God is not willing that any should perish but that all should come to repentance (2 Pet. 3:9) He extends His grace and free gift of salvation. Won't you accept Him today? If you are already a Christian, you prepare for the rapture by living your life for Him and being obedient to His Word—living like He could come back for you at any moment, like His return is imminent because it is! You don't want to be ashamed at His return; see 1 John 2:28 and 3:3. "Looking for that blessed hope, and the glorious appearing of the great God and our Saviour Jesus Christ" (Titus 2:13).

My prayer is that in everything I do and say, I may bring honor and glory to my Lord and Savior and to point people to Him. I fall short of this goal so often, and I am humbled at God's forgiveness, love, mercy, and grace. I have heard the phrase before that *people would rather see a sermon than hear one any day.* I believe that to be true. I close this chapter with another poem that I wrote specifically about the rapture. I pray that it is a blessing and encouragement to you. I pray that it causes you to think and examine yourself regarding your faith.

Are You Ready?

Are you looking for His appearing and ready for His return?
Or are you just going through life without a bit of concern?
His coming is imminent and will occur without delay
Like a thief in the night, but no man knows the day.
In a moment, in the twinkling of an eye,
Caught up together to meet in the sky.
From the grave, the dead in Christ will also rise.
Those that still remain will not believe their eyes.
The Lord will descend from heaven with a shout
To take the bride of Christ on an upward route.
When His church is taken away up into the air,
For those still here, it will be too late for prayer—
Thinking you have time only to find out the hard way.
He's coming back again, and it just might be today.
Once the trump of God sounds, it will be too late.
Now is the day of salvation; please don't wait.
Whosoever will may come, don't be spiritually blind.
Will you trust in Jesus or will you be left behind?

Randy Mlejnek

23

The Health, Wealth, and Prosperity Gospel

There is a very popular message being proclaimed today by some very prominent and well known preachers. It is not my intention in this chapter to call them out individually by name. Rather, I wish to attempt to shed the light of biblical truth on the message they are spreading. Their message, I believe, is a dangerous one that cannot be supported by the scriptures. It is quite simply a distortion of God's Word with an emphasis on selfish desires. It focuses, not on God, but on His blessings and on what he can do for us. This message is known today by several names but is commonly referred to as the health, wealth, and prosperity gospel or the word of faith movement.

In a nutshell, it is the belief that it is God's will for all Christians to be blessed with good health, wealth, success, prosperity, and other earthly temporal blessings. It teaches that these things will be granted to the child of God through their faith, positive thinking, and by their words proclaiming and claiming them. That is why it is sometimes referred to as the "name it and claim it" gospel or "blab it and grab it" and positive confession theology. The emphasis is on our personal happiness. It is the belief that we need not necessarily suffer in this life but that we can speak our desires and the personal destiny that we wish for into existence by our words—that God is beholden to us if we will only have enough faith. It treats our Creator more like a divine genie in the sky that exists to grant our every wish. It is somewhat implied and logically follows in this belief that if you are not successful, if you are not in good health, if you are poor, and if you are not prosperous, you are not right with God and don't have enough faith.

The false teachers that peddle this heresy most often place an emphasis on money in their ministry. They are always asking for you to step out in faith and sow a financial seed to their ministry. They then give the promise that if you do so, you will be rewarded and showered with monetary and other blessings from God many times over than what you gave. It really is nothing more than a religious pyramid or Ponzi scheme. If this really worked, these preachers would be sending you money instead of the other way around. Then, if you send them your money and you do not receive a greater blessing in return, your faith and financial gift was just not great enough. So then, you are urged to really step out in faith and sow an even bigger financial seed. This emphasis on financial giving by prosperity preachers focuses on unscriptural motives as well. They teach that we should give because of what we will get in return, whereas Jesus taught that we should give hoping for nothing in return.

It is not too difficult to figure out that in a pyramid scheme, usually only those at the top of the pyramid are the ones that get rich and reap the greatest benefit. Many of these prosperity gospel preachers fly around in private jets, own multiple luxury vehicles, and live in enormous multimillion dollar mansions. Now, let me be clear. I am not saying that it is a sin to be rich, to have nice things, or to make a lot of money. It becomes a sin when those things become the emphasis and love of your life and, thereby, replace God as your main priority and goal. They then become your idol and what you truly worship. The well-known phrase from the Bible often gets mis-quoted. Money is not the root of all evil, the *love* of money is (1 Tim. 6:10). The last part of that verse often gets forgotten but is equally important to note: "…For which some have strayed from the faith in their greediness, and pierced themselves through with many sorrows."

"I believe that it is anti-Christian and unholy for any Christian to live with the object of accumulating wealth. You will say, 'Are we not to strive all we can to get all the money we can?' You may do so. I cannot doubt but what, in so doing, you may do service to the cause of God. But what I said was that to live *with the object* of accumulating wealth is anti-Christian" (Charles Spurgeon).

"Prosperity teachers insist that worldly wealth, physical health, and material prosperity are the ultimate gauge of how blessed you are by God. Furthermore, they say, you yourself are the one who ultimately determines how much or how little of God's blessings you enjoy. You can manipulate God with your words; you have it within the power of your own heart to summon enough faith to claim whatever blessing you want. And if you are not materially prosperous; if you are sick; if you suffer in any way, YOU are the one to blame because you didn't crank up enough "faith" and create a better reality with a positive confession. You didn't claim your own dream by faith" (Phil Johnson).

Matthew 6:24 tells us that we cannot serve two masters. You cannot serve both God and money. If the prosperity gospel were true, then Christianity really has nothing more to offer this world than what the world itself has to offer. I honestly don't mean to offend anyone reading this who may follow a prosperity preacher, attend their church, or give financially to their ministry. I only wish to point out that this teaching stands in stark contrast to what your Bible teaches. If you disagree with my statement, please don't take my word for it. Search the scriptures for yourself and pray for wisdom and discernment of the truth from the Holy Spirit.

If the pursuit of riches and materially possessions was a worthy goal, don't you think that Jesus would have pursued it? The truth is that He did not do so and did not set that example for us. 1 Timothy 6:9 says, "But those who desire to be rich fall into temptation and a snare, and into many foolish and harmful lusts which drown men in destruction and perdition" (NKJV). The Bible teaches us that we are to be content with what we have (Phil. 4:11). Jesus said that it is easier for a camel to go through the eye of a needle than for a rich man to enter the kingdom of heaven (Matt. 19:24, Mark 10:25, Luke 18:25). Riches can be a dangerous thing, and they are not always a blessing. People have been destroyed by riches and brought to ruin because of them. The goal of wanting to accumulate wealth does not fit in with the biblical teachings of dying to self, to picking up our cross and following Him, or to denying ourselves.

Becoming a Christian does not mean that your life will be worry free and will become all sunshine and roses. We are not guaranteed freedom from suffering. In fact, the Bible tells us that all who live godly will suffer persecution (2 Tim. 3:12). For the Christian, this is not your best life now; your best life is yet to come. Pastor John MacArthur pointed out that the only people who this is truly their best life now are those that are lost and will end up in hell. We are told to lay up for ourselves treasures in heaven (Matt. 6:20). That where our treasure is, there will our heart be also (Matt. 6:21). We are told to seek first the kingdom of God and His righteousness (Matt. 6:33). God does not promise us that all will be good in this life. He promises us in Romans 8:28, "And we know that all things *work together for good* to them that love God, to them who are the called according to his purpose." We are told in John 16:33 that in this world, we will have trials and tribulations.

So instead of the emphasis being on God's blessings and the temporal things of this life, it should be on God Himself. *He* is the goal. He is to be the top priority and to have the ultimate pre-eminence in our lives. When you truly surrender to Him, you will discover that no matter what this life throws at you, He is enough. We are not promised physical health, material wealth, success, prosperity, and a trouble-free life in this world, nor are we to demand it of God.

I close this chapter with a poem that I recently wrote on this topic. Thank you for taking the time to read my ramblings, and I pray that they have been an encouragement to you.

A False Gospel

There is a false message being preached today
that has grown widespread in popularity.
It is a distortion of the scriptures, known as the
gospel of health, wealth, and prosperity.
Its focus is on worldly happiness, while material
possessions and success are the main goal.
But the Bible says, what does it profit a man to
gain the whole world, yet lose his own soul?
The emphasis is on the wrong thing; it's not on God,
but His blessings and what He can do for you.
We should lay up for ourselves treasures in heaven,
not see how much earthly wealth we can accrue.
These false teachers say that you need to give them
your money for God's blessings to unlock.
Living in million-dollar mansions while extorting
the poor, they continually fleece their flock.
This does not produce contentment but covetousness,
so by their words, God's truth they deny.
Ignoring biblical principles, money is their idol;
they try to fit a camel through a needle's eye.
Their ministry is a scam filled with heresy; it's
nothing more than a religious Ponzi scheme.
Feeding lies while they get rich; thousands fill
their churches to listen to them blaspheme.
Beware of these shallow false prophets because
their spirituality only runs skin deep.
They are nothing more than wolves who have
dressed up in the clothing of sheep.
Many struggle to make ends meet while their
pastor's bank accounts continue to inflate.

THE HEALTH, WEALTH, AND PROSPERITY GOSPEL

They attend faithfully seeking help, but all that
they are ever given is an offering plate.
Motivated by the love of money, which is the
root of all evil, they are filled with greed.
Flying around in private jets, with money to
spare, they ask you to sow a financial seed.
They preach that God wants you rich and successful
and that you can have your best life now.
That by faith and positive thinking, you will gain
these things, not by the sweat of your brow.
They tell you to name it and claim it, speak it into
existence; by your words, God is at your beck and call.
I tell you that He is not some divine genie to grant your
selfish desires; He is the King and Lord of all.
Becoming a Christian will not make you rich, guarantee
your health, or that your life will not be rough.
It is about Jesus and His pre-eminence and that no matter
what happens to you here, He will be enough.

Randy Mlejnek

24

Mercy and Grace

Grace and *mercy* are two wonderful words that have such significant meaning to the born-again follower of Christ Jesus. Although closely related and sometimes confused for one another, they are two different things. *Mercy* is not getting something that we do deserve. *Grace*, on the other hand, is getting something that we do not deserve. Grace and mercy are very important biblical concepts that relate to our salvation.

> "For by grace you have been saved through faith, and that
> not of yourselves; *it is* the gift of God (v. 8), not of works,
> lest anyone should boast (v. 9)" (Eph. 2:8–9, NKJV).

The biblical teaching on salvation can be a pretty involved discussion that can encompass many doctrines and teachings. It includes things such as election, predestination, justification, regeneration, sanctification, God's sovereignty, and man's free will—just to name a few. They are all different biblical doctrines but basically make up spokes on the same wheel. The good news is that you *can* know for sure whether or not you are truly saved in this life, and you don't have to be a theologian to understand it all. The salvation that God offers is rich in meaning and spoken of in depth throughout the entire Bible. Some people commit a lifetime of study to soteriology (the doctrine of salvation). Yet its basic concepts are simple enough for a small child to understand.

That is where the core of the Bible's message comes into play—the Gospel or Good News. The Gospel message is summed up rather succinctly for us in 1 Corinthians 15:1–4. Namely, that Christ Jesus died for our sins, that He was buried, and that He rose again the third day, according to the scriptures. Now, just because Jesus died on the cross does not mean that everyone automatically gets to go to heaven. Obviously, there are people that will end up in hell as well. So whether or not you get into heaven is directly related to whether or not you accept God's free gift of salvation.

Make no mistake, though, all roads do not lead to heaven. There are not many ways to get there either, *only one*. That is through Jesus Christ. In John 14:6, Jesus said, "I am the way, the truth, and the life, no man cometh unto the Father but by me." The Bible teaches us that there will be many that will reject Christ and end up in hell for all of eternity. *C.S. Lewis said, "There are only two kinds of people in the end: those who say to God, 'Thy will be done,' and those to whom God says, in the end, 'Thy will be done.' All that are in Hell, choose it..."*

We really contribute nothing to our salvation. It is all of God and all by His grace. I believe in the complete and total sovereignty of God, and I also believe in the free will of man because the Bible clearly teaches both concepts. God is totally sovereign in all things, including our salvation, yet He gives us the freedom to choose or reject Him. He somehow does this in such a way as to remain completely sovereign yet allows us to retain our free will without violating it. I don't know that our finite minds can fully comprehend this as the two concepts seem to be mutually exclusive. There are many scholarly articles written that attempt to reconcile these two biblical teachings. I just know that they are both true.

I don't claim to be able to understand or explain everything about God. That is why He is the Creator, and I am the creation. Why worship a God you can fully explain anyway? The infinite, eternal, omniscient God is beyond our mind's ability to fully comprehend. What I know of Him and His character, I know from His Written Word. From there, I know that He is completely holy and just and that the Judge of all the earth will do right. So I fully trust in Him even though I may not be able to fully understand or explain Him; that is where faith comes in.

The Bible teaches that we are saved by God's grace through faith. It has nothing to do with our good works (Eph. 2:8–9). That is an unbiblical and erroneous belief that many people have. That at the end of this life, your good works will be weighed against your bad works, and if you have more good works than bad, you get into heaven. That is a lie from the pit of hell. You can't earn your way to heaven. If we could earn our way there, Jesus Christ would not have had to come and die for us.

We are all sinners (Rom. 3:23) who rightly deserve the wrath of God for our sin. When you accept God's free gift of salvation, you do not receive His wrath, but His mercy. Instead of His wrath, you get clothed in the righteousness of Christ Himself. That is God's grace. Grace is unmerited favor. You can't earn it, and you don't deserve it. Grace and mercy are kind of like two sides of the same coin. Mercy is showing compassion toward someone whom it is within your right and ability to punish or harm.

> "Not by works of righteousness which we have done, but according to his mercy he saved us..." (Titus 3:5, KJV).

Everything that we learn about God, His nature, and His characteristics, come from His written revelation to us. The Bible teaches us many things about Him. We know that He is an infinite, eternal, all-powerful being. We also know that God cannot act contrary to his Word or His character. We know that God is love according to His Word. Some may wonder, since God is a God of love, then why can't He just let us all in to heaven. The answer is because the God of the Bible who is infinitely loving, rich in mercy, and full of grace, is also infinitely holy. He is a holy, just, and righteous God who cannot allow sin to go unpunished.

So we are all sinners; I think most people would be willing to admit that. The Bible teaches us that our sin separates us from God. We are fallen sinful creatures who deserve death in hell. People, many times, try to compare themselves to others at this point. They think that they are not really that bad of a sinner because they have never murdered or raped anyone. That is a natural human tendency to compare ourselves with other people. The problem is that you may not be "as bad" as your next-door neighbor morally, but they are not the standard of measure whereby we are judged. We are judged according to God's sinless perfection. The truth is that we all fall way short of that standard.

So we are separated from a holy, sinless, and perfect God by this wide canyon because of our sin. This divide is not a gap that we can bridge ourselves. We are dead in our trespasses and sins, the Bible says (Eph. 2:1). Even what we would consider our good and righteous works are considered as filthy rags (Isa. 64:6). We are lost and in desperate need of saving.

You see, God, because of His justice and holiness, cannot just overlook sin. He can't just sweep it under the rug and sneak us in the back gate of heaven. If He were to do that, He would not be a righteous or a just judge. He must pronounce us as guilty because of our sin. We deserve to pay the penalty for our sin; we are guilty. That is where God's grace and mercy come into play.

God, because of His love, extends the grace and mercy of the cross. He bridges that canyon of separation between us with the cross. He entered His own creation in the form of man to provide Himself as the sacrifice to pay the penalty for our sins. While we were yet sinners, Christ died for us. God's love, mercy, grace, justice, holiness, and His wrath all come together and meet at the cross of Calvary. He who knew no sin, became sin, that we might be made the righteousness of God in Him (2 Cor. 5:21). What manner of love the Father has bestowed upon us that we should be called the sons of God... (1 John 3:3). For you know the grace of our Lord Jesus Christ, that though He was rich, yet for your sakes He became poor that you through His poverty might become rich (2 Cor. 8:9). He left the glories of heaven to come down to this earth. He humbled himself and became a man. He endured the suffering and the shame to demonstrate His love for us and to make a way where there was no other way. He paid a debt He did not owe because we owed a debt we could not pay. Wow, that is enough to make even a backslidden Baptist shout!

My words couldn't possibly or adequately express the wonder and the love expressed through God's grace and His mercy. I encourage you to read His Word and think about His love for us and how He demonstrated it toward us at the cross. If you have never accepted God's free gift of salvation and entered into a right relationship with Him, I pray that today would be the day that you do. I could not say it better than the two old hymns state it:

"Amazing grace how sweet the sound that saved a wretch like me. I once was lost, but now I'm found, was blind but now I see."

"Mercy there was great, and grace was free; pardon there was multiplied to me; there my burdened soul found liberty... at Calvary."

I close this chapter with a poem that I wrote about mercy and grace. I pray that it would be an encouragement to you.

Grace and Mercy

God's grace is the power source that flows through faith's conduit.
Each element is vitally necessary to reap salvation's benefit.
It is not by your good works or effort as
stated in Ephesians 2:8 and 9.
You are saved by grace through faith, when
the two of them combine.
It's not by works of righteousness which we have done,
But according to His mercy, made possible by the Son.
Though He was rich, yet for your sake, He became poor.
Washed in His blood, your sins He will remember no more.
Christ paid a debt He did not owe because
we had a debt we could not pay.
Grace and mercy come into focus when the
wonders of the cross you survey.
His holiness demanded justice, and sin's
penalty needed to be fully satisfied.
Jesus paid it all! Through His blood and
sacrifice that has been supplied.
It's at the cross of Calvary, where God's
justice, grace, and mercy all meet.
And with His resurrection, His perfect plan
of redemption was complete.
Grace is receiving a blessing we *do not*
deserve—in short, unmerited favor.
Mercy is not receiving what we *do* deserve;
from sin's penalty, we get a waiver.
When Satan makes his accusations and points his finger at our face,
We have an advocate with the Father, and
it's He who pleads our case.

He shows His nail prints and reminds the
devil that He died in our place.
Clothed in *His* righteousness, that—my
friend—is His mercy and His grace.

Randy Mlejnek

25

Heaven

An intriguing question that almost everyone has contemplated, whether they consider themselves to be religious or not, is this: When a person dies, will they live again? This question was posed in Job 14:14. Is there life after death? One thing is certain about this life—we all die. The moment that we are conceived, the aging process begins. We all have a limited amount of time in this life. It matters not how much money is in your bank account, how many earthly possessions you have accumulated, what your social status is, how high up the corporate ladder you have climbed, or what level of power or influence you have attained. One hundred years from now, none of that will matter. We all eventually die and our bodies will turn to dust.

So is this life all there is? The moment that you take your final breath and your heart stops beating, do you then cease to exist, or is there life beyond the grave? Is there a conscious existence beyond this physical world that we experience with our senses? If so, what is it like? Pondering these questions and thinking about death is not a comfortable subject for many people. It forces you to recognize your own mortality. Life is fragile, and in the grand scheme of things, it is very short. The Bible says that life is but a vapor that appears for a short time and then vanishes away (James 4:14). Nobody is promised tomorrow.

Maybe you have had a loved one pass away recently, or have attended someone's funeral. The topic of life and death is fresh in your mind, and you might be struggling with some of these very questions yourself. I would like to try to convey to you some of the truths in God's Word that relate to this subject. The Bible very clearly teaches that there is life after death. This life is not all there is for us.

The clear teaching of the scripture is that the moment you die, your soul is instantly transported to one of two places—either heaven or hell. The Bible does not teach any sort of soul sleep, purgatory, complete annihilation, or reincarnation. You die, then you either go to heaven or hell for all of eternity. If you die and end up in hell, your fate is sealed, and you can never get out. For the Christian, the Bible teaches that to be absent from the body is to be present with the Lord (2 Cor. 5:8). The Bible teaches that both heaven and hell are literal and physical places, not just a state of mind. The doctrine of hell or eternal punishment is a topic for another day. For the remainder of this chapter, I wish to focus on life eternal in the presence of the Lord in heaven.

So, what is heaven going to be like? The Bible says, "But as it is written, eye has not seen, nor ear heard, nor have entered into the heart of man the things which God has prepared for those who love him (1 Cor. 2:9, NKJV). Philippians 1:23 says that being in heaven with Christ is "far better" than being here on the earth under the curse of sin. If you look at the imperfect world around us with all of its beautiful scenery, sunsets, and topography, you can imagine that heaven will be even more wonderful beyond our wildest dreams.

Paul was given a glimpse of heaven while he was still alive in a vision. He writes of this experience in 2nd Corinthians chapter 12. The Lord, however, did not allow him to detail the things that he beheld with his eyes. In the book of Revelation, God allowed the apostle John to get a glimpse of heaven in a vision as well. He does attempt to express to us from that vision the sheer beauty of heaven (Rev. 21). He writes of gates of solid pearl, architecture made from precious jewels, a crystal sea, streets of gold so pure that they are transparent like glass, a magnificent flowing river, fruit bearing trees. This celestial city is said to have twelve foundations that have the names of the twelve apostles written on them. The Bible says that it has twelve gates, each of which has written on them the name of one of the twelve tribes of Israel.

When most people talk about heaven, they are referring to what is known as the present heaven or in theological circles as the intermediate heaven. It is that place where the soul of Christians go when they die to await their bodily resurrection. It is the dwelling place of God in a perfect environment and where His throne is. Yes, we will be given a new resurrection body someday. It will be an incorruptible body, without sin, sickness, disease, death, or the many other limitations of our current earthly bodies.

All that we know of heaven, we learn from the Bible, God's Word. There is, however, much that we simply don't know. In addition to that, there are also many misconceptions and wild speculations out there that we see on television or in the movies that have no scriptural basis.

In the Bible, the word heaven is used to describe primarily three different places. We read of the first heaven in Genesis 1:1: "In the beginning, God created the *heavens* and the earth." Heaven here is used to refer to the sky or the earth's atmosphere. In other places, it refers to the stars, outer space, and the universe. "The *heavens* declare the glory of God; the skies proclaim the work of His hands" (Ps. 19:1). And lastly, heaven is also referred to in the Bible as the dwelling place of God. This is the "third heaven" that Paul speaks of in 2 Corinthians chapter 12. He said that he was "caught up" to this third heaven. That is the heaven that I would like to very briefly talk about.

The exact and precise location of God's central dwelling place in the present (intermediate) heaven is unknown to us. The Bible does not give us a set of coordinates or a map of where it is. It does reveal to us how to get there, but not exactly where "there" is. The location of the future heaven is given to us, and the Bible says that it will be on the new earth that God prepares.

This intermediate heaven is a place without pain or suffering, but it is not the final place that we will dwell forever. The Bible teaches that at the end of human history, at God's appointed time, He will come down to dwell among His people in a new heaven and a new earth (Rev. 21, 22). Some scholars refer to this as the eternal state. It will literally be heaven on earth. We will dwell with God on this earth, but it will have been divinely "remodeled" if you will. It will be perfect, as when He first created it, before the curse of sin came upon it. The capital city of this heaven on earth will be the New Jerusalem. This city is alluded to in various places in the biblical text, but most in detail in Revelation chapter 21. It is called different names too: the holy city, the celestial city, the city foursquare, etc. We are given the dimensions of this city as being 1,500 miles cubed! It will be illuminated by the light of the glory of God Himself.

We will have our resurrected bodies, and we will live and reign with Him forevermore. There will be no more sin, sorrow, death, pain, wars, or conflict. We will one day live in this perfect environment, with perfect resurrected bodies—bodies that won't have the same physical limitations that we currently have. The last time God dwelled with man in a perfect environment on this earth was in the Garden of Eden before the fall.

In Revelation chapter 22, it tells us that there will be a river running through the new heaven, and on each side of the river, there will be trees—Much like there was in the Garden of Eden. There will be water, trees, fruit, and food to eat. We will be able to communicate and have conversations with others there. There is nothing in the

Bible about floating around on a cloud for all of eternity, strumming a harp in boredom. Heaven is going to be a magnificent place with such amazing beauty. It will literally be a perfect environment in the presence of our creator God, where we will worship Him and experience joy and pleasure beyond anything our human minds can currently comprehend.

If you would like to do more in-depth reading on this topic, I would recommend a book by Chip Ingram titled *The Real Heaven*; it is published by Baker Books, (2016). I close this chapter with a poem that I wrote on heaven. As always, I pray that it will be an encouragement and a blessing to you.

Heaven

There will be no more pain there, no more
death, and no more night,
No more crying or need for candles, for the Lamb will be the light.
Our hearts can't imagine its beauty, eye
has not seen nor ear has heard.
Of the place prepared for those that love
Him, according to His Word.
It is the dwelling place of the living God
and contains His very throne.
John was given a glimpse, and in a vision,
its splendor he was shown.
The true reality of heaven, words cannot adequately express.
Access will be exclusive, and it has very strict code of dress.
Your good works won't matter or who you managed to impress.
It's reserved only for those that are clothed in His righteousness.
One day, heaven will be made new and
brought down to this earth—
A brand new city for those who have experienced a spiritual rebirth.
Gates of pearl, your own mansion, and a
street of gold as clear as glass.
Like Eden restored, before Eve was deceived
by that snake in the grass.
A majestic river flows, and on both sides,
trees that bare 12 kinds of fruit.
At death, you are transported in an instant;
it won't be a long commute.
Contrary to popular belief, Saint Peter does
not control entrance through the gate.
Whether you accept Jesus and His offer of
salvation, that is what seals your fate.

HEAVEN

Architecture that's made out of precious jewels
and what appears to be a crystal sea.
Angels proclaim holy, holy, holy, Lord God
Almighty, who was, and is, and is to be.
Abraham, Isaac, and Jacob, the saints of old will all be there.
To reign with Him forever in that glorious city built foursquare.
The only thing made by man will be the
scars in our Savior's hands and feet.
For me, the best part of heaven will be
when face to face my Jesus I meet.

Randy Mlejnek

26

Sola Scriptura

One of the most important foundational principles of the Christian faith is known by the Latin phrase, *sola scriptura*. It means "scripture alone." It came to become the mantra of the sixteenth-century Protestant Reformation. Its primary meaning has to do with the belief that scripture alone is fully sufficient to be the ultimate and final authority on matters of faith, doctrine, salvation, the church, and all religious and spiritual practices. There is no other authority that is greater to or even equal with it. It was born in contrast to religious institutions that were upholding erroneous unbiblical doctrines, practices, and man-made traditions as being equal to or even of greater authority than the scriptures themselves, primarily the Roman Catholic church.

If God truly does exist and He created us—and I believe that He does and He did—He would certainly have the ability to communicate a message to His creation. I believe that He did communicate a very clear message to us as a divine written revelation contained in the Bible. God transmitted that message to us according to His sovereign will through the medium of written language, using human agents to do so as they were "carried along by the Holy Spirit" (2 Pet. 1:21).

The Bible is truly a miraculous book that has stood the test of time and was given by the inspiration of God Himself. It declares that *all* scripture is given by inspiration of God and is profitable for doctrine, for reproof, for correction, for instruction in righteousness. That the man of God may be perfect (complete), thoroughly furnished or equipped unto all good works (2 Tim. 3:16–17). That word *inspired* is a translation from the Greek meaning literally "God breathed" (theopneustos). The Bible is the very Word of God and as such it is truth. It is inspired, infallible, inerrant, eternal, unchanging, and all-sufficient. This is the consistent testimony of the scriptures. You see in the writings of the prophets over and over again, "thus saith the Lord," and in the writing of the apostles, "it is written."

It is precisely because the Bible alone is divinely inspired, literally God breathed, that it must stand above any other authority. It is by the perfect rule of scripture that everything else must be weighed and measured. No church, document, doctrine, institution, individual, council, decree, dogma, or tradition can trump the written Word of God. The canon of scripture is the final and highest authority. That word *canon*, meaning rule, standard, or measuring stick, is often used to describe the scriptures. It is an authoritative collection of books (The sixty-six books of the Bible). The Bible is also what is considered a closed canon. It can't be added to or taken away from; it is complete. There is a dire warning given for anyone who would add to or take away from the Bible (Rev. 22:18–19, Deut. 4:2, Deut. 12:32).

Now, *sola scriptura*, scripture alone, does not mean scripture only or scripture in isolation (*solo* scriptura), nor does it claim that all truth of every possible kind is contained in scripture. There are obviously some things and scientific truths that the Bible does not address. The Bible contains all truth that is necessary for our salvation, faith, godly living, and spiritual matters. The scriptures are the supreme authority on all matters that they address. Obviously, there is other authority and truth out there. Much can be learned from church history and from reading the writings of the early church fathers. It can be profitable to study the early Christian creeds and traditions, but they must all be judged by what the scriptures say. If they run contrary to the Word of God, they must be rejected. The Bible is that perfect, eternal, and universal standard of measure that we must weigh everything against.

Without *sola scriptura*, all you have is man's fallible opinion that has the final say and your doctrine and theology have no solid foundation whatsoever to stand upon. There are those that teach and believe in *sola ecclesia*, or the church alone, as having the final authority on religious matters. They hold to unbiblical traditions and man-made doctrines that run contrary to the Bible's teaching. This must be rejected as heresy, and God's Word must be at the top of the authority food chain. All religious practices, doctrine, and traditions must be measured against the rule of scripture.

Now, *sola scriptura* as a term or phrase came into being during the sixteenth-century Reformation, but its principle has been taught and believed by many since the scriptures came into existence. Jesus even taught that the traditions that the Jews of His day believed and practiced were to be subjected and, if need be, corrected by scripture (Matt. 15:1–9).

So we know that not only has God truly spoken to us in His written word, but we learn from it that He also desires a relationship with us too! I wonder, do you know Him personally today? He did not just create us and then leave us all alone in the dark to fend for ourselves. He gave us a guidebook to learn about Him and to be a lamp unto our feet and a light unto our path (Ps. 119:105). God desires a personal and intimate relationship with His people. That relationship is to be entered into by grace through faith in the atoning work of Christ. It is to be marked by a life of obedience to His Word—fervent, continual, and consistent prayer—and in the believer, being a faithful ambassador of Christ by proclaiming and spreading the Gospel message. All while pursuing a life of holiness as a living sacrifice and immersing themselves in the scriptures. God empowers the believer for this relationship and their tasks to follow by His indwelling Holy Spirit. It is constantly guiding, convicting, and conforming them ever more into the image and likeness of His Son, that they may know Him and the power of His resurrection, all the while accomplishing His perfect will, furthering His kingdom, and bringing glory and honor to His name.

It all comes down to your view of the Bible. You either believe that it truly is, as it claims to be—the inspired, God breathed, eternal, inerrant, infallible Word of Almighty God—or you don't. Even if you don't, that does not change the fact of reality that it is indeed truly that. As such, it is and should be the Christians ultimate final authority on matters of faith, salvation, doctrine, and practice. There can be only one ultimate and supreme authority. Your religious beliefs, doctrines, traditions, practices, and personal conduct, should be viewed through the filter of the lens of scripture, and not the other way around.

I hope I've helped you to see the importance of *sola scriptura* and the dangers of trying elevate anything else to a level of authority above scripture. God has clearly spoken to us in His Word, the Bible. I encourage you to read it, study it, and to seek a closer more intimate relationship with our Lord. Again, I have merely scratched the surface of a topic that can be deeply expounded upon. I don't have the time or, quite frankly, the educational background to qualify me to go much more in depth than what I have. If you would like to learn more about this subject, I would highly recommend reading a book by James R. White titled *Scripture Alone*. I close this chapter in my typical fashion, with a poem that I wrote about the topic I discussed. I pray that it will be a blessing and an encouragement to you.

Sola Scriptura

It was the battle cry that was born out of
the 16th century Reformation
To counter unbiblical traditions in favor
of holding to divine revelation.
It is the solid foundation upon which all the
pillars of our faith firmly stand,
A universal standard of measure that doesn't
change or move like shifting sand.
Doctrine, practices, and beliefs must all
be tested by this divine source.
Done the other way around, is putting the
doctrinal cart before the horse.
Step off its foundation, and you will find yourself
standing on a theological banana peel.
Add to or take away from His Word, and I can
assure you that the consequences are real.
Based upon the truth, this principle is the
only way to avoid subjectivity.
There is no higher rule or equal weight we
are to use to govern our activity.
The Bible stands on its own as the only
truth that is divinely guaranteed.
In matters of supremacy, it sits at the pinnacle,
nothing else can supersede.
It is eternal and can't be outranked or
overridden; it is our final authority.
Hold fast to the Latin phrase of *sola scriptura*,
nothing else can take priority.
Don't base your religion merely upon
traditions, opinions, or how you feel

Because operating outside the scope of
Scripture will be your Achilles's heel.
Stray from it, and you will find yourself sliding
down a very steep slippery slope.
No church, dogma, decree, institution, or
council can trump it, not even the pope.
Let nothing else have the final say, and stick
only to this divine measuring rod.
That is the all-sufficient, inerrant, inspired,
infallible, Word of Almighty God.
You can't cover up the scent of heresy by
spraying it with religious cologne.
It will be revealed when compared to truth
and that is through scripture alone.

Randy Mlejnek

27

Be Bold and Courageous

Have you ever had an impromptu opportunity arise to be able to share your faith and to be a testimony of God's amazing grace, but you kept silent? I know that I have squandered opportunities and let them slip away. Times that I should have taken the opportunity to speak up, but I did not. Probably most of you can relate to this. Maybe it was out of the fear of offending someone who you know did not hold to the same beliefs as you? Maybe it was because you felt inadequate and unprepared to defend and articulate your position biblically in a conversation? Maybe it was out of a concern of being mocked or laughed at in a group setting for actually holding to such an unpopular position amongst a group of coworkers?

Speaking up and sharing our faith with others who are outside our Christian circle of friends can be a very intimidating and daunting task. It's easy to be bold in your statements in a Bible study amongst like-minded individuals at church, in your small group, or in a Sunday school class. It is another story altogether to share those statements outside that setting, where you are likely to encounter opposition to those views. I have been presented with opportunities where I felt that small still voice and urging of the Holy Spirit within me to share the Gospel with others, yet embarrassingly, my lips stayed shut.

I believe that we need to be bold and courageous in sharing our beliefs and in living out our faith on a daily basis in a consistent manner. Presenting the Gospel and making disciples is not just the pastor's job. We are all called to do it. Now, I am not talking about being rude, obnoxious, or forcing your beliefs down someone else's throat. We are called to speak the truth, but we need to do so in love. That is not always an easy thing to do with something that we are so passionate about. Sometimes, we Christians can get carried away and can end up pushing someone further away from the truth because of how we present it. It is possible to speak the truth in an unloving and offensive way. We need to be wise as serpents yet harmless as doves.

Consistency is another important aspect of our Christian faith. This is an area in my own life that I have failed at miserably over the years. Remember, people are watching you. Your life may be the only Bible that some people ever read. You have heard the phrase, people would much rather see a sermon than hear one any day. What message are you "preaching" with your life? Do you go to church on Sunday, but then live like the devil the rest of the week? How do you conduct yourself when you are treated unfairly, wronged, or faced with adversity? Your Christian testimony is especially important during those times.

One piece of advice I would give to others about being bold and courageous to share your faith is to be prepared. Have your ever been unprepared for something? Maybe a speech, an exam at school, a meeting, or presentation at work? Being fully prepared makes all of the difference. Being prepared brings with it confidence and boldness. So how does that translate to the topic at hand? I believe it starts with knowing your Bible. We are told in 2 Timothy 2:15, "Study to shew thyself approved unto God, a workman that needeth not to be ashamed, rightly dividing the word of truth" (KJV). In 1 Peter 3:15, it says, "But sanctify Christ as Lord in your hearts, always being ready to make a defense to everyone who asks you to give an account for the hope that is in you, yet with gentleness and reverence" (NASB).

I am not saying that you have to be a seminary graduate or a theologian to share your faith. You should study the Bible, however, because as a Christian, it should be *the* basis and solid foundation for your faith. Know why you believe what you believe, especially about critical doctrines of the faith. If someone were to ask you why you became a Christian or simply how to become a Christian, you should know how to articulate the answer to those questions. If you are not sure how best to answer those questions, then prepare. I would encourage you to write out your testimony in your own words of how you came to know the Lord, practice it, and commit it to memory. Learn and memorize the relevant scripture passages that deal with sin and salvation. As Christians, we should be saturating our minds with the Word of God.

> "You shouldn't place God third down on your priority
> list, only spend about five minutes a day with him,
> treat Him as an afterthought, and then expect him
> to move mountains for you" (Randy Mlejnek).

Another part of being prepared is prayer. Pray for courage and boldness to share your faith. Ask God to help you to prepare and for opportunities to cross your path for you to do just that. This may be a huge obstacle for you to overcome. It could just be that you are a shy person. Talk to the Lord about this, and share your concerns with Him. With God, all things are possible (Matt. 19:26). Spending time with the Lord every day in prayer can give you the confidence and boldness that you need. Are you spending time with the Lord daily? You shouldn't place God third down on your priority list, only spend about five minutes a day with him, treat Him as an afterthought, and then expect him to move mountains for you.

We can be bold in our prayer life too. Hebrews 4:16 tells us to come boldly to His throne of Grace. Sharing your faith does not have to be a sixty-minute dissertation on every major doctrine in the Bible and the origins of the universe. It can be as simple as handing out a Gospel tract to your waitress when you pay your bill after a meal out. Actively look for opportunities to present the Gospel. If you are a Christian and you have never done this before, I encourage you to commit to doing so. Attempt to share Jesus with at least one person in the next thirty days. Take the time to prepare, study, and pray for God's guidance in this endeavor.

Allow God's love and light to shine forth through your life (Matt. 5:16), and try to cultivate and develop a relationship with that neighbor or acquaintance that you know doesn't go to church. Allow them to see a difference in your life and be willing to help them when you see a need that they have. Sooner or later, the opportunity will probably present itself, and you will be able to share what has made the difference in your life.

When was the last time that you invited someone to come to church with you? Do the people that you know, outside of your congregation, and those that you work with, even know that you are a Christian? I read part of an article on boldness, and it said that we should be "unveiled, unashamed, and unambiguous" with others about our faith and about the One in whom we put our trust. Again, not beating people over the heads with the Word of God, but uncompromisingly speaking His truth *in love*. Be bold and courageous and remember that you are not alone; you have the Holy Spirit of the living God inside of you. There is a song by Jeremy Camp called "Same Power" that really drives this point home.

I close this chapter with a poem that I wrote on being bold and courageous. As always, I pray that it will be both a blessing and an encouragement to you.

Be Bold and Courageous

I want to speak the truth always, in love, yet
uncompromisingly and without fear,
To stand boldly for the Lord, even in adversity,
like Peter when he cut off Malchus's ear,
Like Elijah, on Mount Carmel, when he called
down fire and defeated the prophets of Baal,
Like the disciples who proclaimed the Gospel in
Acts chapter 5 even after being thrown in jail,
Like the prophet Nathan who confronted David
about Bathsheeba and the wickedness of his sin,
Like the two spies with a good report that the land
could be taken and the battle they could win,
Like all of the apostles who went to their graves
preaching the truth having died a martyr's death,
They stood boldly for Jesus, the risen Savior, spreading
His message up until their dying breath.
Like Gideon who was vastly outnumbered and yet
he boldly went to battle with only 300 men,
Like Daniel who refused to obey the king's decree
not to pray and was thrown into a lion's den,
Like the courage of Esther who went before the
king for her people, risking her own demise,
Like Rahab the harlot who, in her home in the city
of Jericho, helped hide the Israelite spies,
Like Joseph, who refused to compromise his
integrity when tempted by Potiphar's wife,
Like Abraham who courageously followed God's
command to place Isaac under his knife,
Like the Hebrew children who refused to bow down
to Nebuchadnezzar's statue made of gold,

Then thrown into a fiery furnace, yet they were
unharmed; it must have been a sight to behold.
Like the young shepherd boy who stood bold and
courageous, armed with only stones and a sling,
David stood fearless as he defeated Goliath the giant,
then later to become Israel's mighty king.
Like Paul preaching with zeal, though persecuted,
shipwrecked, beaten, arrested, and stoned,
This world could be turned upside down for Christ
if his passionate boldness could be cloned.
God told Joshua "be strong and courageous" as he
would lead His people into the Promised Land.
The Bible says the righteous are bold as a lion, trust
the Shepherd, don't be afraid to take a stand.
We often seem to forget though, as Christians, we
are tapped in to the same power source.
We need to be bold and courageous with our eyes
fixed on Jesus, faithful to stay the course.

Randy Mlejnek

28

Voiceless Victims:
the Issue of Abortion

The topic of this particular chapter is most certainly a divisive issue. The decision made by the United States Supreme Court in the Roe v. Wade case of 1973 indelibly altered the political landscape of this country. Politicians running for positions in local elections all the way up to the office of the Potus have been divided on this issue. Just the mention of this topic can create hostility between two otherwise calm and rational individuals with opposing viewpoints. People feel very strongly in their stances on both sides of this controversial issue. I am one of those people.

I have chosen to write about this topic not to create friction, nor to intentionally offend. Although the very divisive nature of this issue just about makes that an inevitability. However, as a Bible-believing Christian, I believe that I cannot just stay silent about something of this magnitude. God's Word is crystal clear as to the sanctity of human life. I personally believe that abortion is murder, and it goes against God's commands. I believe that life begins at conception. Also, for the record I am equally opposed to any violence perpetrated against abortion doctors and clinics in the name of the pro-life movement or otherwise. There is no doubt in my mind that the legalization of abortion was the thread that was pulled that has done more to unravel the moral fabric of this nation than anything else before it.

There have been over 50 million babies slaughtered, dissected, and pulled from their mother's wombs since 1973. Thousands of innocent children are intentionally murdered every day in this country at the hands of abortion doctors. How these "doctors" justify their actions against the Hippocratic Oath that they take to preserve human life defies logic. I have read articles for and against abortion. I have listened to viewpoints from both sides. I could quote endless statistics to you or even try to shock your conscience with detailed descriptions of how barbaric the different abortive procedures are.

The truth of the matter is that my opinion is probably not going to change your mind if your viewpoint differs from mine. If the undercover Planned Parenthood videos of this past year did not open your eyes to the pure evil and wickedness of the abortion industry, your conscience is probably already seared. If all of the advancements in medical technology that have shown us the amazing images and video of the early development of these tiny humans hasn't swayed your opinion, I'm sure that your mind is made up. If you will not listen to and follow the clear teaching of scripture on this issue, certainly, my thoughts on the subject will have little to no impact on you. I do truly encourage you to take a step back and to take a deep hard look at this issue. I sincerely urge you to reconsider your position. Seek God's Word and what He has to say about human life.

If your thoughts and opinions on this issue are the polar opposite of mine, I don't hate you. In fact, I am commanded in God's Word to love you. You are entitled to your opinion. I don't view myself as morally superior to you in any way. I am a sinner just like everybody else in this world. I do have to speak the truth to you, but I endeavor to do so in love. Maybe you have had an abortion yourself. If so, I want you to know that God loves you and can and will forgive you if you ask Him to. Your sins no more condemn you than anyone else's. We all fall short of God's perfection. The blood of Christ that He shed at Calvary can cover all of your sins.

If you happen to agree with me on this issue, I urge you to pray for our nation and those in authority. Exercise your right to vote men and women into office who will stand upon biblical principles, values, and morals. Always speak the truth uncompromisingly, but do so in love. You will not change any minds or win anyone to Christ by "beating" them over the head with your Bible. Ultimately, I think that this is a heart issue. The scriptures tell us that the heart is deceitful above all things and desperately wicked (Jer. 17:9). Until God changes a person's heart, we can't expect their behavior or thoughts to change. Share the gospel and allow Christ's love and light to shine through your life to others.

If you happen to be on the fence on the abortion issue, I urge you as well to seek God's face and what His Written Word has to say on the subject. Read Psalm 139:13–16, Jeremiah 1:4–5, Psalm 51:5, Luke 1:39–44 for starters.

"The Bible contains numerous references to the unborn. Each time the Bible speaks of the unborn, there is reference to an actual person, a living human being already in existence. These Scriptures, taken in context, all indicate that God considers the unborn to be people. The language of the text continually describes them in personal terms. Since the Bible treats those persons yet unborn as real persons, and since the development of a person is a continuum with a definite beginning at the moment of fertilization, the logical point at which a person begins to be human is at that beginning. The answer is that life begins at conception (using the now older definition of the term, here to be synonymous with fertilization). Frankly, no other conclusion is possible from Scripture or science" (www.answersingenesis.org).

God's Word teaches that before He even formed us in our mother's womb, He knew us. God told Jeremiah that before he was born, he sanctified (set him apart) him. John the Baptist leaped for joy in his mother's womb. Life and personhood begins at conception. Unborn babies are not just clumps of cells one minute and then magically as they pass through the birth canal become a human life, a person.

I encourage you to go to YouTube and search for a video called *Matt Chandler on Abortion*. It is a six-minute video clip excerpt from a sermon he preached called The Sanctity of Human Life. Please take the time to watch this powerful video after reading this chapter. This video was a motivational factor in the poem I wrote below. I leave you with a poem I wrote on abortion.

Voiceless Victims

They are not just tissue or tiny clumps of cells.
They are a life, God's creation, just like the Bible tells.
They are not to be dissected, and their parts
sold so someone can be paid.
They bear the image of the Creator; they are
fearfully and wonderfully made.
Millions have been murdered all across this very land.
At rest now with the Savior, they are in the Father's hand.
This is the Gospel inverted—no longer "I died for thee."
But for the sake of convenience, you will die for me.
You take an innocent life and say that it's just a choice.
If only they could speak, but you never give them a voice.
Sacrificed on the literal altar of self, the abortion doctor kills.
How do they sleep at night and not wake up with chills.
Technology has given us a glimpse inside the womb.
The baby recoils in pain as it meets its final doom.
If you listen closely, their very blood cries out.
They would choose life; of this, I have no doubt.
A human life cut off, never given a chance to bloom.
A heart stopped from beating, never to resume.
Citing a majority vote in Roe v. Wade,
The convictions of others you try to persuade.
Trusting in men's wisdom, you are completely fooled.
The Supreme Court of heaven has you overruled.
How do we cure this evil? Is there a vaccine?
I believe one can be found in 2 Chronicles 7:14.
We have called good evil, and evil we have called good.
Look to Calvary, where Jesus died on a cross made of wood.

Randy Mlejnek

29

Deliberately and Intelligently Designed

The next time you are out and about look around, what do you see? Perhaps the beautiful sight of the sun setting or the twinkling of countless millions of stars against the dark and vast backdrop of space. An eagle soaring effortlessly in the clear blue sky or that undisturbed fresh snow covered blanket across the ground first thing in the morning. The breathtaking colors of a Michigan fall across the landscape. A field of wild flowers with every color of the rainbow dancing in the wind or the waves of the ocean, gliding across the sand of the shoreline. Perhaps even a thundering waterfall or a pure ice-capped mountain cresting into the clouds. The endless beauty of the sights and sounds of this world that we live in are astounding.

Now consider for a brief moment how all that visual and auditory bliss is processed by your senses. The sights and sounds of your environment are received through your eyes and ears among other senses. Signals are transmitted to your brain, where they are processed, interpreted, and perceived. Take for a moment if you will the complexity and intricacy of the human eye. Even the self-proclaimed evolutionist Robert Jastrow, in his 1981 book *The Enchanted Loom*, once wrote: "The eye is a marvelous instrument, resembling a telescope of the highest quality, with a lens, an adjustable focus, a variable diaphragm for controlling the amount of light, and optical corrections for spherical and chromatic aberration. The eye appears to have been designed; no designer of telescopes could have done better. How could this marvelous instrument have evolved by chance, through a succession of random events?" Even though a firm believer in evolution, Jastrow confessed that "…there seems to be no direct proof that evolution can work these miracles… it is hard to accept the evolution of the eye as a product of chance."

To think that all of what we see and what we are, with all of the complexity and obvious fine tuning, somehow happened by sheer random chance through some cosmic explosion billions of years ago is a tough pill to swallow intellectually. To borrow a line from the title of a book I own by Norman Geisler and Frank Turek, "I don't have enough faith to be an atheist." You could never get the perfect order and harmony of what we have today from something as chaotic as an explosion or a "big bang." I think it takes more faith to believe in evolution than it does to believe in a God who created all things. As I have heard the statement before, you could never get an encyclopedia from an explosion in a paper factory.

Consider the following illustration that has been around in this debate for many years. Although I do not know who to attribute it to, I will try to articulate its concept in my own words. From my understanding, the average Rolex watch is made up of around one hundred to two hundred different parts. They all have to be put together in a certain order and in exacting precision in order for the watch to work and keep time properly. Say you were to take every one of those individual parts, every screw, spring, and unassembled little metal piece, and placed them in some sort of a tumbler and shut the door. Then, you spin that tumbler with those watch parts for millions and even billions of years. When you opened the door on the tumbler, that watch would not be perfectly assembled and keeping time. It would take a deliberate and intelligent designer to put that watch together. Maybe you disagree with me and think that given enough time, those watch parts could be perfectly assembled, you still would have to explain where the watch parts themselves came from to begin with. Some evolutionists would argue that this example is not a fair or accurate comparison, but I think it encapsulates the essence of the belief in evolution. In contrast, consider the makeup of the human body. We contain way more parts than a Rolex watch and we are infinitely more complex and intricate. For our bodies to function and work the way that they do requires such precision and fine tuning to such exacting specifications. Just the human eye alone, as I alluded to earlier, is an engineering marvel in and of itself. Now, consider the complexity of the entire universe!

Yes, I believe that everything was deliberately designed and created by the eternal God. If you believe that, as I do, it is not hard to also believe that the all-powerful Creator was able to communicate a written message to us and to have His words recorded and then preserved for us down through the ages. Yes, I also believe the Bible is the Word of God and that it is true. I think that is also why the most contested and attacked portion of the scriptures is the first eleven chapters of the book of Genesis. It is the foundation for everything that follows. If you could disprove and do away with Genesis 1–11, the rest of the entire biblical narrative would crumble. "Every single Biblical doctrine of theology, directly or indirectly, ultimately has its basis in the book of Genesis" (Ken Ham, *The Lie: Evolution*). The most widely read, studied, debated, and dissected book in all of history, the Bible, has never been proven to be false, though many have tried.

I believe the creation account as it is explained in the first book of the Bible. I believe in a literal six-day creation because that is what I believe the Bible teaches. I also believe that the earth is not billions of years old either. I believe that it is probably less than ten thousand years old. These details of the biblical creation account are also debated and are a topic of discussion for another day. Some resources that I would recommend if you wanted to dig deeper into this study for yourself would be The Institute for Creation Research (www.icr.org) and Answers in Genesis (answersingenesis.org). I would also recommend the writings of Ken Ham and Dr. Henry Morris, the founder of ICR as well as the Henry Morris Study Bible.

Creationism is an incredibly interesting subject to study. My father-in-law has studied it for a long time and is quite knowledgeable about it. He has probably forgotten more about it than I have ever learned. He is captivating to listen to as he articulates his biblically based beliefs on the topic. One of the best Sunday school series I ever sat through was one that he taught on creationism and the differing world views related to it. "Atheism is so senseless. When I look at the solar system, I see the earth at the right distance from the sun to receive the proper amounts of heat and light. This did not happen by chance" (Isaac Newton). We live in a fine-tuned universe that was deliberately and intelligently designed by our Creator, the eternal God of the Bible. I close this chapter with a poem that I wrote on the topic of creationism. I pray that it is a blessing and encouragement to you.

Creation

In the beginning, God created; that is what I believe.
Not in an instant, it took six days for Him to achieve.
On the seventh day, He rested but not because He needed sleep.
It was an example for us to follow and one He wanted us to keep.
All part of the Master's plan and by His deliberate design,
The heavens declare His glory and mighty power divine.
He placed the sun and stars perfectly in the sky.
And divided the water from the land that was dry.
He spoke light into existence and separated the day from the night.
He made all the animals on the earth and the birds that take flight.
He made the trees, flowers, and moon that shines in the dark.
He made us in His own image, and we bear the Maker's mark.
God's power throughout the works of His
hand are amazingly displayed.
We are the crowning of His creation; we are
fearfully and wonderfully made.
He made the angels and the streets of gold in
heaven, where my feet will one day trod.
What manner of love He has bestowed on us
that we should be called the sons of God.
Look all around you; the wonder of His majesty is on display.
For those who refuse to believe, your excuses are taken away.
From the mountains, to the valleys, and all the fish in the sea.
The mysteries of creation can be unlocked, He is the master key.
He is before all things, and by Him, all things consist.
Your theory of evolution and the Bible just can't coexist.
You were not there, and your thoughts on
our origin are pure speculation.
My understanding comes from the eternal
God and His written revelation.

This world did not come to be by an explosion billions of years ago.
It was designed by our Creator, who made
all things, above and below.
Only through the lens of scripture can
we make sense of what we see.
It was not by random chance, but because of His sovereign decree.

Randy Mlejnek

30

God's Word: Handle with Care

I enjoy reading, and there is nothing like a good book to stimulate your mind and stir your emotions. A skilled author can create such vivid and colorful mental imagery in our minds eye that no Hollywood movie blockbuster can replicate. There is one book, however, that is completely unique from all others in existence. Not only is it the best-seller of all time, but the author is God Himself, and that book is the Bible. Of all the words ever penned, only one book was written by the Almighty. I've heard it said that reading the Bible is like thinking God's thoughts after Him. That is a pretty deep and powerful thought if you dwell on it for a moment.

The divine providence that went into the formation of that book along with the blood that has been shed by faithful men and women who helped distribute and compile it leaves me in awe. That the Creator of the universe wrote a love letter to his creation and then preserved it down through the ages so that we could hold a copy in our hands is truly a miracle. Yet how many of us have a Bible, or several of them for that matter, that just sit on the shelf and collect dust? God only wrote one book, and most of us own a copy. Yet we don't spend time reading it, learning from it, and allowing it to guide us. I challenge you to read it through from cover to cover if you have never done so. It is not so daunting of a task if you just bite off small portions each day. There are plenty of Bible reading plans out there, find one that suits you and ask God to reveal Himself to you as you read through and study His Word.

Of all the books ever written, the Bible is most certainly the most misused, abused, and taken out of context. So many have twisted its plain meaning to fit their personal agenda. I've heard it said that the Bible is not a bag of trail mix, you can't just pick out the pieces that you like and ignore the rest.

We need to handle the Word of God with care, to study it, and to make sure that we are rightly dividing the word of truth (2 Tim. 2:15). When you start adding to it or taking away from it, you are standing on quickly sinking sand. Adding personal opinions to it or isolating verses out of context to build an entire doctrine around are dangerous waters to venture into. Let God's Word speak for itself and let His Holy Spirit guide you into all truth (John 16:13). Let scripture interpret scripture and allow the plain meaning of the text to come through.

Now, I know what you might be thinking at this point. You may be saying to yourself that there are countless numbers of highly educated, godly, and competent biblical scholars, and even they don't all agree on the meaning of every passage of scripture. I understand that, and I realize that there are some more difficult passages of scripture and none of us has all of the answers. There will always be some level of disagreement among God's people on issues of doctrine and theology. That is not what I am talking about here. I am referring to those that blatantly mishandle God's Word to preach hate, to advance a personal agenda, or those who twist its meaning to try and justify their sinful behavior.

You can make the Bible (or just about any other book or document) say just about anything by doing one simple thing—taking things out of context. A quick Internet search gave me a very simple definition of context as it applies to our current discussion here.

"The parts of something written or spoken that immediately precede and follow a word or passage and clarify its meaning." In the biblical text, that is the verses that precede the one that you are reading and the ones that follow, along with the biblical narrative as a whole. Remember, every text has a context. Don't try to read something into a passage of scripture that isn't there. Bible scholar Ron Rhodes has a policy when it comes to biblical interpretation. He says, "When the plain meaning of the text makes good common sense, seek no other sense, lest you end up in nonsense." I think that is good advice to follow. Remember, when it comes to proper biblical interpretation, context is king. Taking a passage out of context is the easiest way to misinterpret what a passage is actually saying.

We also have to remember that the Bible was written using human language and so it contains metaphors, similes, allegory, hyperbole, personification, typology, symbolism, and other figures of speech. There are also different literary genres in it: poetry, history, proverbs, apocalyptic, wisdom, personal letters, law, etc. I heard a pastor answer when asked if he takes the Bible literally, respond by saying that he takes the Bible correctly. It is important to identify the type of literature you are reading in any given passage. If you don't account for this, and you take every word literally, you might think that God is a bird with wings and feathers because Psalm 91:4 says, "He shall cover thee with his feathers, and under his wings shalt thou trust..."

Generally, however, I believe that we should take the Bible literally and at face value for what it says unless the particular passage and its immediate context dictates otherwise. I believe people find themselves on theologically unstable ground when they try to spiritualize and allegorize every passage of scripture looking for some hidden meaning as they try to read between the lines.

I remember in the Bible college that I attended, they had a course in hermeneutics. It is basically the study, principles, and methodology of interpretation as it pertains to the biblical texts. There are a number of different principles involved in proper biblical interpretation. They include, but are not limited to, looking at the context of a passage, identifying the kind of literature you are reading, making sure that you interpret the passage correctly by considering the historical background and culture at the time the text was written, and applying proper grammatical principles.

One more quick thing to consider when reading, studying, and interpreting the Bible is the two major approaches. There is the exegetical approach and the eisegetical approach. One of the clearest explanations of the difference between exegesis vs. eisegesis that I found online was from a website called gotquestions.org.

"Exegesis and eisegesis are two conflicting approaches in Bible study. Exegesis is the exposition or explanation of a text based on a careful, objective analysis. The word exegesis literally means 'to lead out of.' That means that the interpreter is led to his conclusions by following the text.

The opposite approach to Scripture is eisegesis, which is the interpretation of a passage based on a subjective, non-analytical reading. The word eisegesis literally means 'to lead into,' which means the interpreter injects his own ideas into the text, making it mean whatever he wants. Obviously, only exegesis does justice to the text. Eisegesis is a mishandling of the text and often leads to a misinterpretation. Exegesis is concerned with discovering the true meaning of the text, respecting its grammar, syntax, and setting. Eisegesis is concerned only with making a point, even at the expense of the meaning of words."

Well, I have only just scratched the surface of what there is to be learned regarding proper biblical interpretation and Bible study. I have much to learn myself, and the more I learn, the more I realize I don't know. I hope that I have possibly sparked an interest for you to dig deeper into this topic and into God's Word. His book to us is so deeply profound and applicable to our lives, especially in the twenty-first century.

I heard someone say once that you could intensely study the Bible for an entire lifetime and still not fully mine the depths of its richness. I close this chapter with a poem that I wrote regarding handling the Word of God with care.

Handle with Care

God's Word is not a bag of trail mix; you
don't just get to pick and choose.
You can't just take a verse out of context to
make it fit your personal views.
Both believers and unbelievers are guilty
of this on both sides of the aisle.
Twisting the meaning of the text to suit their
needs, they are living in denial.
It is hypocritical for someone to only
selectively obey God's Holy Word.
It is so inconsistent when they only follow
the parts that are preferred.
Some mishandle the scriptures in order to hold
people down with a legalistic weight.
They attempt to impose rules and standards, not
from God, but ones that they create.
There are those with itching ears who will
only listen to what they want to hear.
They won't endure sound doctrine, and unto
fables and myths, they will adhere.
Some know the name of Christ but haven't
experienced His saving grace.
Without the Holy Spirit to correct their
errors, blatant lies they will embrace.
Some seek additional revelation and wish to
keep the canon of scripture open.
His Word is complete we are told not to add
to it, for God has already spoken.
When it comes to proper biblical interpretation, context is the king.

Isolating verses to build a doctrine around
them is a dangerous thing.
So in order to avoid changing God's Word and
to ensure His truth you rightly divide.
Use a sound exegetical approach, and make
sure proper hermeneutics are applied.
He didn't leave us to figure it out all on our own
but sent a comforter to come alongside.
Don't rely on personal opinion but through prayer,
allow the Holy Spirit to be your guide.

Randy Mlejnek

31

Marriage, Soul Mates, and Valentine's Day

As I write this, it is almost Valentine's Day. I thought a post on marriage would be fitting. Marriage is an extremely important institution created by God. It is a deeply integral part of my faith and belief system that I feel strongly about. Considering the current culture, trends, and the laws of the day, this chapter may raise some eyebrows. Just because an issue is controversial does not mean that it should not be talked about. I believe that people can have opposing views (even about politics, religion, or morality) and still have a productive and friendly dialogue. You are free to disagree with me if you like, and I will respect your right to do so.

So to have a commentary on marriage, I believe I must first define it or at least try to articulate its parameters. Not by what the current and recently changed laws of this country say it is, but defined by the one who created the institution, the eternal God who never changes. The biblical view of marriage is a permanent covenantal union, in relationship, between one man and one woman (husband and wife) till death do they part.

As a disclaimer, this is not an anti-gay personal opinion piece to see how many people I can offend. This is also not me trying to hide behind religion or the Bible to preach a message of hate, quite the contrary actually. I don't hate anyone. If you are gay, I don't hate you. In fact, my Bible commands me to love you. I may personally disagree with your lifestyle, but I do not hate you. My personal belief, based on the teachings of scripture, is that marriage is to be between one man and one woman. That is not a popular thing to believe or say in today's culture, but I believe it nonetheless.

Now, I know that at this point there are many side trails that this topic of discussion can take. Some people may say that it is just my interpretation of the Bible that brings me to those conclusions. I think that the Bible speaks very clearly on this issue and you are free to disagree with me. It is not my intent to address the specific biblical texts or to debate their meanings in this post. If you want an excellent scholarly work on that subject from a biblical standpoint, I would recommend that you read James R. White's book, *The Same Sex Controversy*.

Now, having said all that, I don't view myself as morally superior to you if you disagree with me on what has always been the biblical traditional view of marriage. Why would I, because you sin differently than I do? I believe, as the Bible teaches, that we are all sinners (Rom. 3:23). Unfortunately, I think that a great many people do hide behind the guise of religious beliefs to preach hate. For some reason, many times in evangelical circles, homosexuality gets elevated as if it belongs in some special category of greater sins. If you are gay and have been mistreated by an over zealous "Christian" because of your sexual preference, let me just tell you that I am sorry. People that preach hate are not acting in obedience to what scripture teaches and they are wrong. We are supposed to speak the truth, but we are to do it in love.

You will never see me condone the type of actions that the unfortunately infamous Westboro Baptist Church takes with their hate-filled, anti-gay rhetoric. The protesting that they do at the funerals of many of our military men and women who died in combat just because they happened to be gay is deplorable. Those brave men and women deserve our respect and people who protest a military member's funeral for those reasons should be ashamed.

Yes, it is true that in the United States of America in 2016, you are legally allowed to marry another person of the same sex. The Supreme Court of the United States has completely redefined the institution and boundaries of marriage. I recognize those facts; I don't personally agree with them, but I do acknowledge them. I also believe that just because something is legal, does not make it right. I disagree with abortion being legal in this country as well, and I wrote a previous chapter on that topic if you want to read it. If a same sex couple were to come and visit my church, I would not treat them any differently than any other visiting couple. I would be one of the first to greet them with a handshake, and they would be more than welcome to sit next to me and my family on the pew. I believe that my pastor and the congregation of my church would show genuine, Christlike love and care for them as well.

If you are gay and you are my neighbor, if I work with you, or if we are simply riding an elevator together, I will not shun you or look down upon you. I will not disrespect you. I will not teach my kids to hate or shun you either. I do believe that it is my responsibility to teach my children biblical truths and values. Those would include loving your neighbor as yourself as well as the biblical view of marriage. Those that hold strictly to the Bible's clear teaching on this issue sometimes get labeled as being intolerant or anti-love. I feel that in order to herald a message of tolerance, it can't be paired with intolerance for views that happen to disagree with your own. For those who are dogmatic in their stance on this issue, can't we just respectfully agree to disagree?

Now that I have expressed my belief in the biblical view of marriage and my desire to be free to express that view, let's move on to another angle in this topic of discussion. I want to touch on this belief that many people have in soul mates. This has been a topic of much debate within Christian circles. The arguments seem to center around God's perfect will and His permissive will. Thoughts seem to vary on this issue, depending on how you define the term "soul mate." It seems to be more of a cultural buzzword that isn't always clearly defined. The following is a quote from a blogger I enjoy reading by the name of Matt Walsh: "We've got it all backwards, you see. I didn't marry my wife because she's The One, she's The One because I married her. Until we were married, she was one, I was one, and we were both one of many. I didn't marry The One, I married this one, and the two of us became one." That quote is from an interesting post he wrote on marriage and soul mates. Author Gary Thomas says, "The most common misconception Christians have about marriage is finding a 'soul mate' — someone who will complete us. The problem with looking to another human to complete us is that, spiritually speaking, it's idolatry. We are to find our fulfillment and purpose in God… and if we expect our spouse to be 'God' to us, he or she will fail every day. No person can live up to such expectations."

I think the entire soul mate issue gets used as an excuse for infidelity when things aren't going perfectly in one's marriage. They think that because things aren't all sunshine and rainbows in their marriage, their spouse must not be their true soul mate. All of a sudden, they begin talking to that friend or co-worker who just seems to understand them and they naively assume that they must be their one true soul mate. Hence, entertaining these erroneous beliefs many times leads to adultery followed shortly thereafter by divorce. So whatever your belief on the soul mate issue might be, for the Christian who is married, it is forsaking all others, till death do you part. So this Valentine's Day, remember that your spouse is *the* one and needs to be the *only* one. They are now not only your *soul* mate, but also your *sole* mate.

I do not claim to be a marriage expert; I am far from it. I am by no means the model husband. I have made more than my fair share of horrible choices in my marriage. I have only been married once, and I am still married to my beautiful bride since 1999. I would like to share a few things that I have learned over the years. Marriage is not something to be entered into lightly. It is a very serious commitment. A good marriage takes hard work, trust, patience, dedication, and the ability to forgive. No matter how rocky the road is that your marriage has been down, with God's help, He can heal and restore it. My wife is my best friend and truly a gift and a blessing from God. We have hit some major bumps in the road along the way, but by God's grace we are still together. God is making something beautiful out of our lives and in our marriage, despite the bumpy road of our past.

If I could recommend one book (besides the Bible) to help enrich your marriage for you and your spouse to read together, it would be *The 5 Love Languages* by Gary Chapman. My marital advice in a nutshell would be to make the Lord the centerpiece and focal point of your marriage. Beyond your personal relationship with God, you should make your marriage your first priority. Learn to forgive each other quickly and don't hold a grudge. Pray together and for one another. Continue to date each other even after you are married. Don't lie! Once trust is broken, it is a very hard thing to get back. Communication is key; talk to each other, and do it respectfully. Protect and guard your marriage at all costs. Set in place in your marriage solid boundaries and hedges of protection to guard against external temptation. Giving in to temporary pleasure can lead to permanent regret. I close this chapter with a poem that I wrote on the topic of marriage. I believe that there are some great biblical truths and principles contained in it that can help strengthen your marriage.

Marriage

Great marriages don't just happen, nor are they created overnight.
They take hard work, sacrifice, and you have to be willing to fight.
The commitment is not to be taken lightly; it's till death do us part.
You have to give it your everything and love with all your heart.
It is not a 50/50 relationship, it is 100 percent from each.
Success will not come easy; it is not a walk on the beach.
Don't go to sleep angry or let the sun go down upon your wrath.
You have to be willing to forgive and walk united on the same path.
Put a hedge around your marriage, and guard it with your life.
For it is a sacred bond, the one between husband and wife.
Don't be deceived into tasting forbidden fruit,
For the food from that tree has a poisonous root.
The grass is not always greener on the other side.
The grass is greener, where the water is applied.
Temptations will come along and knock at your door.
Run from them; don't walk. These curiosities don't explore.
The institution was created by God; He gets to define the terms.
It is between one man and one woman, of this the Bible reaffirms.
Your life is no longer your own; what was two becomes one flesh.
It is a new journey you travel together, a life you get to start fresh.
The other person's needs should come before your own.
They now take first place; yourself you must dethrone.
You no longer walk alone; side by side, you are a team.
Always show respect and hold them in highest esteem.
The relationship is a symbol of Christ and
the church, His only bride.
Are you willing to sacrifice as He did? He
laid down His life and died.

Randy Mlejnek

32

The Paradox of Christianity

Merriam-Webster's Dictionary defines the term paradox as "a statement that is seemingly contradictory or opposed to common sense and yet is perhaps true; a tenet contrary to received opinion." *The Cambridge English Dictionary* defines paradox as "a statement or situation that may be true but seems impossible or difficult to understand because it contains two opposite facts or characteristics."

The Christian life is, at its core, an amazing paradox. It is filled with statements, values, and principles that, on the surface, seem totally illogical and senseless. Things that run contrary to modern thought and that are looked down upon as plain foolishness by the unbelieving world. If you were to go to your local Barnes and Noble bookstore and flip through the self-help books, you would probably find none of them that matched the recipe for daily living that the scriptures lay out.

In God's Word, we are told to love our enemies, to bless those that curse us (Matt. 5:44). We are told we need to die in order to truly be able to live (Gal. 2:20). We have to lose in order to gain, to surrender in order to experience victory. We are to be last in order to become first, to make ourselves low and humble in order to be lifted up and exalted. God says that He will use the weak to overcome the strong and the foolish things of this world to confound the wise

(1 Cor. 1:27). We need to learn to serve in order to be able to lead (Matt. 20:26). We are told to lose our life if we wish to keep it. We are told to rejoice when we suffer persecution (Matt. 5:11–12). We are to die to ourselves, to take up our cross, and follow after Him. To die to our own fleshly lustful desires and to seek after God's will and not our own. To present our bodies as living sacrifices for His glory (Rom. 12:1). What kind of a "life coach" would give out that advice? The answer is the very Creator, Giver, and Sustainer of life Himself, that's who. As nonsensical as some of those statements might seem to you, there is no other life that can compare to the Christian life.

The fulfillment, joy, and peace that a born again child of God can experience through a relationship with Jesus Christ passes all understanding. Now, I am not saying that living a committed, separated, and obedient Christian life will solve all of your problems and make all of your troubles disappear. In fact, the Bible tells us that if we live that kind of a life, we can expect trials, troubles, and persecution in this world (2 Tim. 3:12). Life is full of trials, troubles, and difficulties, and no one is totally exempt from that. The difference is that we, as Christians, have the Lord God Almighty right by our side to guide us through the storms that will come our way.

The Bible says greater is He that is inside of me than he that is in the world (1 John 4:4). Christianity is the only religion in the world where a man's God comes and lives inside of him. That is truly an amazing thought when you really sit back and ponder it. Worldly wisdom will tell you to take all that you can get out of life. If you have to step on others along the way, so be it, but you make sure to get yours. Only the strong survive, survival of the fittest. The world looks at weakness and dependence on someone else as a disadvantage.

In Christianity, it is just the opposite. His strength is made perfect in our weakness (2 Cor. 12:9). Pastor Alistair Begg has said, "If dependence upon God is the objective, then weakness is an advantage." The world says that the Bible and Christianity are just a crutch for the weak... Yep, it is! I am weak, and I need Jesus. Without God, I am nothing. What does it profit a man to gain the whole world and yet lose his own soul (Mark 8:36)? The late missionary Jim Elliot once said, "He is no fool who gives what he cannot keep to gain that which he cannot lose."

Yes, Christianity is full of paradoxes. It goes against the grain of "worldly wisdom." I will, however, choose to take God's Word over man's word every time. Call me weak and mock me if you want to, but I will keep leaning on my Savior. As a song I enjoy called "I Can't Even Walk" by Southern Gospel Revival says, "...Down on my knees I'll learn to stand. I can't even walk without You holding my hand..." I close this chapter with a poem I wrote that I titled *The Paradox of Christianity*.

The Paradox of Christianity

We must be willing to surrender if we wish to be freed.
We must first learn to serve if we ever intend to lead.
We are made strong when we are weak.
To be lifted up, we must be lowly and meek.
We find our life by losing it; we live by dying.
Taking up our cross and our own flesh denying.
We have to give in order to receive.
We glory in trials instead of grieve.
The first shall be last, and the last shall be first.
To everyone else, these roles should be reversed.
God is one, yet united in a community of three.
Father, Son, and Holy Spirit—blessed Trinity.
We are to love our enemies and turn the other cheek.
To bless those that curse us and not of them evil to speak.
Though He was rich, for our sake, He became poor
That through His poverty we could have riches galore.
God has chosen the foolish things of the
world to confound the wise.
The natural man can't understand this, no matter how hard he tries.

Randy Mlejnek

33

Prayer Changes Things

*"We may not be able to fully explain why God has ordained
prayer as a vehicle whereby He works in the world, or
how prayer works. Nevertheless, Scripture is unmistakably
clear that prayer does effect objective change."* *

Prayer really does change things and we should be availing ourselves
of this great privilege that God has blessed us with. We have been
given 24/7 access to the Creator of the universe. That is a pretty
amazing thought if you really think about it. The Bible says that we
can come boldly to the throne of grace in Hebrews 4:16. We are told
to pray without ceasing in 1 Thessalonians 5:17. We are commanded
to pray in many places throughout the scriptures, one of which is in
Colossians 4:2. We personally have direct access to God in prayer
through Jesus Christ. We don't have to go through a preacher, pas-
tor, priest, rabbi, or any other member of the clergy, or any other
person (alive or dead) to get to God. The Bible says that there is one
mediator between God and man and that is the man Christ Jesus (1
Tim. 2:5). No ordinary man, whatever title or office he may hold,
can absolve you of your sins. We know from the teaching of the Bible
that Jesus was no ordinary man, but He was God in the flesh. The
second member of the triune Godhead. He was completely human

and yet completely God, possessing both natures (a theanthropic being). Only God can forgive sins.

1 John 1:9 says, "If we confess our sins, he is faithful and just to forgive us our sins, and to cleanse us from all unrighteousness" (KJV). The Bible tells us not to come to God in prayer with iniquity in our heart, unconfessed sin in our life. Having unconfessed sin in your heart will hinder your prayer life (Ps. 66:18). This includes forgiving others of their trespasses against you (Mark 11:25-26, Matt. 6:14–15). Prayer is essential to our Christian walk. You see Christianity, as taught in the Scriptures, is not so much a religion, as it is a relationship. A relationship with the God of the Bible is what it is. How many people do you have a relationship with that you never talk to? God says that if we draw near to Him, He will draw near to us (James 4:8).

When is the last time that you got down on your knees and really earnestly prayed for your spouse, your marriage, your children, a family member, or friend in need? Prayer is of critical importance in a Christian's life. You have to be tapped into the power source, which is God. The late Leonard Ravenhill used to say that a man is never greater than his prayer life. I believe that to be true. The Bible says in James 5:16 that the prayer of a righteous person is powerful and effective (NIV).

Prayer changes things. I've watched it happen first hand. I am where I am today because of a mother and wife who faithfully prayed for me and who continue to do so. Prayer needs to be a part of our daily lives. Jesus set the example for us in that He prayed regularly. C. S. Lewis said, "God designed the human machine to run on Himself. He Himself is the fuel our spirits were designed to burn, or the food our spirits were designed to feed on. There is no other." We need prayer and a personal relationship with Jesus Christ! I admit that I do not pray nearly as much as I should and it is easy to come up with excuses and reasons to try and justify that. With all of the commands in the Bible to pray, the example of Jesus Himself, and the awesome privilege of being able to pray anywhere at any time, is there really a viable excuse not to spend more time in prayer? I try to pray every day and ask God to guide and direct my every step, my every thought, my every action, my every spoken word, my motives, and my attitude. You can't truly live the Christian life in your own power and strength. You have to depend on God and draw from His strength. The sooner you learn this lesson, the better. His grace is sufficient, His strength is made perfect in our weakness (2 Cor. 8:9). "If dependence upon God is the objective, then weakness is an advantage" (Alistair Begg).

God does not always answer our prayers in the way that we wanted. God is not some divine genie in the sky at our beck and call to give us everything that we want or ask for. "Prayer is not the means by which we obtain everything that we want. It is the means by which God draws us closer into the pattern of what He wants us to become" (Ravi Zacharias). Prayer changes more than just circumstances; it changes you. Prayer is not just asking for things either. You may be familiar with the prayer model as outlined in the acronym A.C.T.S. It has been around for a long time and is based on the different types of prayer that are given to us in the Scripture. I do not know who originally came up with this acronym to give them their proper credit, but it looks like this:

A: Adoration (worship)
C: Confession (of specific sins)
T: Thanksgiving (gratitude)
S: Supplication (specific requests)

That is a good prayer model to follow that can help get you started if you have no idea how or what to pray. Our prayers are usually answered in one of three ways—yes, no, or wait. God's timing is not always the same as our timing, keep praying. God is much wiser than we are, and He knows what is best for us. God's wisdom goes beyond the ability of human beings to fully comprehend it. It reminds me of a lyric from a song entitled "Unanswered Prayers" by country singer Garth Brooks. He said that some of God's greatest gifts are unanswered prayers. Some of the things that we pray for that we thought that we needed or just wanted to happen that didn't happen could have been a blessing in disguise.

I've heard more than one preacher use this next saying in their sermons. They ask, why is it that the Wednesday night prayer meeting is always the smallest in attendance? It goes something like this, "If you want to see how popular a church is, come on Sunday morning and see how many people are there. If you want to see how popular the pastor is, come back on Sunday night. If you want to see how popular God is, come back on Wednesday night for the prayer meeting." We have lost sight as Christians of the power and importance of prayer. You can pray anywhere at any time. You don't have to be on your knees with your eyes closed or facing a certain direction. Prayer is not a position, it is a disposition. I do it when I am driving (eyes open) all the time. You bow your heart in submission to God and talk to the Almighty. There is nothing wrong with getting on your knees, bowing your head, and closing your eyes out of reverence to a holy God. I do those things as well at times when the situation allows for it.

Robert Browning had this saying about prayer that I think really helps put things in their proper perspective on this issue. He said that when he sees children ride a mock horse, he is tempted to embarrass them and tell them that their stick is a mock horse and that they really are carrying what they say carries them. When a child takes that stick and pretends it is a horse and rides it, Browning is saying it is a mock horse, and they are actually carrying what they say carries them. Ravi Zacharias speaking on Browning's mock horse illustration said this, "If you are a praying Christian, your faith in Christ will carry you. If you are not a praying Christian, you will have to carry your faith and you will get exhausted bearing the infinite."

I close this chapter with a poem that I wrote on prayer. I hope that it is a blessing to you. Remember, seven days without prayer makes one weak. Have you talked to God today?

My Daily Prayer

You are the potter, and I am the clay.
Mold me and make me, Lord Jesus, I pray.
My prayer each day right from the start
Is that I don't regard iniquity in my heart.
Let your love and light shine through my life.
Watch over and protect my kids and my wife.
I present my body as a living sacrifice.
I am not my own; I was bought with a price.
Help me to produce the fruit of the Spirit,
And may I proclaim your word for all to hear it.
Help me to forgive and turn the other cheek
And to resist temptation when I am weak.
Thank you for your love, mercy, and grace.
To seek your will is the goal that I chase.
Forgive my sins and grant me spiritual health.
And help me to love my neighbor as myself.
Let my motives be pure and my words be true.
May I glorify your name in all that I say and do.

Randy Mlejnek

* See John Munro, *Prayer to a Sovereign God*, Interest 56:2 (February 1990):20–21. Thomas L. Constable, *What Prayer Will and Will Not Change*, in Essays in Honor of J. Dwight Pentecost, pp. 99–113.

34

The Apostle Paul: from Murderer to Missionary

Thirteen of the New Testament's twenty-seven books were written by him. They are the following: Romans, 1 Corinthians, 2 Corinthians, Galatians, Ephesians, Philippians, Colossians, 1 Thessalonians, 2 Thessalonians, 1 Timothy, 2 Timothy, Titus, and Philemon. Many biblical scholars believe that he also wrote the book of Hebrews, but we just don't know for sure. His story is quite amazing. He went from being one of the most violent enemies of Christianity to one of its biggest champions. He went from massacring Christians to becoming a missionary. He went from being a persecutor of the church to becoming persecuted himself. He went from being a murderer to being a martyr. That man is of course the apostle Paul. He is introduced to us in the biblical text first as Saul of Tarsus.

It was somewhat common custom in Paul's day to have dual names. It appears from scripture that he was known by both Saul and Paul (Acts 13:9). Shortly after his conversion, he was thereafter referred to by the name Paul in the scriptures, seemingly by his own choosing. God changed several people's names in the Bible, but Paul does not appear to be one of them. There is no reference in the Bible of Jesus changing Saul's name to Paul. The name Saul is typically associated with his role as a persecutor of the church before his conversion and the name Paul is that which is typically associated with his post conversion life.

He was from Tarsus in the Roman province of Cilicia. This would be modern day southern Turkey. He studied under the well-known teacher and Pharisee, Gamaliel, a member of the Sanhedrin, the Jewish ruling council. Paul was well versed in the Hebrew scriptures and Jewish law and religious customs of his day.

So what was it that turned this oppressor of the bride of Christ into a convert? What turned him so suddenly from a murderer to a missionary, persecutor to preacher, religious terrorist to righteous teacher, from crisis to the church to crucified with Christ? It was none other than a miraculous personal encounter with the resurrected Savior. Paul was on his way to Damascus to imprison, persecute, murder, and wreak havoc on the Christians there. Yet in Galatians 1:15–16, we read that it pleased God to reveal Jesus Christ to him. That is grace! God delights in saving his children. You think that you have so messed up your life that God could not possibly use you? Paul said that he was the chief of sinners, (1 Tim. 1:15), yet God's grace transformed him. He was used to turn the world upside down for God's glory.

This sudden and complete 180-degree transformation of Paul the persecutor to his subsequent faithful service to the Christian faith is one of the most solid evidences for the fact of the resurrection of Jesus Christ from the dead. That someone could go from one extreme to the other so quickly is astounding. Someone who was so dogmatically opposed to Christianity being moved to proclaiming its message all over the world simply can't be explained any other way. He had a real encounter with the risen King, and he was gloriously saved. He went to his death, proclaiming the Gospel until his last breath. He suffered greatly for the message he preached, yet he never wavered. He was beaten with rods, arrested and thrown in prison, bound with chains, stoned, whipped multiple times, shipwrecked at sea. He went hungry at times, yet he kept the faith, ran the race, and fought a good fight. With everything that Paul suffered, he never ceased to preach the Gospel of Jesus Christ. Yet, how often do we hesitate to share our faith with others for fear of much less?

Paul also performed many miracles during his lifetime. He healed the sick and the lame, he cast demons out of people, and he even raised a man from the dead. A man by the name of Eutychus was listening to Paul preach late into the night. He went to sleep and then fell out of a third story window and died. Paul went down to him and laid his hands on him and raised him back to life. God enabled Paul to have extraordinary powers of healing. In Acts 19:11–12, it says, "Now God worked unusual miracles by the hands of Paul (v. 11), so that even handkerchiefs or aprons were brought from his body to the sick, and the diseases left them and the evil spirits went out of them (v. 12)" (NKJV). He survived a poisonous snake bite once and then proceeded to heal every sick person on the island where he was shipwrecked (Acts 28:8–9).

Paul mentions a "thorn in the flesh" in 2nd Corinthians 12:7. A great many scholars have attempted to give their thoughts on exactly what they think that this thorn in the flesh was. The fact of the matter is that we just don't know. Many speculate that it may have been some type of a chronic eye or vision problem. None of us can say for certain what it was, but it was no doubt a source of pain and discouragement in Paul's life. Paul asked the Lord multiple times to remove it, but He would not. We are told the reason for God allowing this thorn in Paul's flesh, however. It was given to Paul to keep him humble. (2nd Cor. 12:7) Instead of removing it, God gave His sufficient grace and showed Paul that His strength is made perfect in weakness.

I have heard it said of Paul's thorn in the flesh that a possible reason we are not told specifically what it was may be for our benefit. That possibly God wanted this difficulty in Paul's life to be unknown so that we could apply it to any trial or difficulty that we may face. It was described in such general terms and with enough ambiguity that we could apply the lessons Paul learned from his difficulty to our own lives. For us it could be physical, emotional, or spiritual, yet we can say like Paul that no matter the trial we might face, His grace is all sufficient for us. Full and complete dependence upon God is one of the keys to living the Christian life and therefore our weaknesses can be an advantage.

Paul knew the grace of God well, and he wrote about it in many of his epistles. I like what he said in 2 Corinthians 8:9, "For ye know the grace of our Lord Jesus Christ, that, though he was rich, yet for your sakes he became poor, that ye through his poverty might be rich" (KJV).

G.R.A.C.E.
God's
Riches
At
Christ's
Expense

If we could only have the passion and zeal of Paul to depend fully on the Lord and live a dedicated and committed life to Him. If we truly gave Him total control of our time, talents, and treasures, the tremendous difference it would make in our lives. I trust that you know and have experienced God's saving grace in your life today. I close this chapter with a poem that I wrote on the apostle Paul. As always, I pray that it will be a blessing and an encouragement to you.

The Apostle Paul

He was from Tarsus in Cilicia, and persecuting
Christians was his primary mission,
Having them arrested and even killed and he
did so with great zeal and ambition.
He was there when the first Christian martyr was
killed, and he watched as Stephen was stoned.
He was keeping the coats of the men that killed him,
and this unjust murder he happily condoned.
He was well versed in Jewish tradition, and he
studied under the great teacher Gamaliel.
As to the law, he was blameless, and concerning
the Hebrew Scriptures, he knew them well.
He was a Pharisee of the Tribe of Benjamin,
a scholar, and a tentmaker by trade.
He wanted to stamp out Christianity; this was
the purpose of his unholy crusade.
He was known by many for his violence and
oppression while others just knew him as Saul.
After the reference to his other name in Acts 13:9,
he was always referred to in Scripture as Paul.
His entire life was changed in an instant while
traveling one day on the Damascus road.
He had an encounter with the resurrected Lord,
and upon Paul a new mission He bestowed.
In this miraculous vision of the risen Savior, he was
changed and temporarily blinded by the light.
Under the divine inspiration of the Holy Spirit, almost
half of the New Testament he would write.
He even wrote scripture, known as the prison
epistles, while in Rome under house arrest.

At that time, he made it clear in Philippians that
the joy of the Lord is what he possessed.
An ongoing battle rages within the believer as their
old and new natures simply don't mesh.
Being a Christian does not guarantee a trouble-
free life, even Paul had his thorn in the flesh.
He said God allowed this to keep him humble, so
as not to exalt himself or to get a big head.
Pride must have been a temptation with all of his
miracles; he even raised a man from the dead.
Some of his most famous words were, "I can do all
things through Christ who strengthens me."
Teaching power for the Christian life comes from
God, and total dependence upon Him is the key.
He planted churches and preached, traveling the
Roman Empire on three long missionary trips.
During this time, he penned thirteen letters and
proclaimed the Gospel of Christ with his lips.
He fought a good fight, he finished the race, and
it is believed that he died a martyr's death.
He never wavered, while proclaiming salvation and
Jesus's resurrection until his dying breath.
One of the greatest lessons that we can learn from
the life of Paul and his transformation
Is that no one is beyond the reach of God's
amazing grace and His offer of salvation.

Randy Mlejnek

35

How Is This for a Resumé

Have you ever prepared a personal resumé in hopes of attaining employment in a particular job or position? If so, you probably compiled a listing of your educational background, personal qualifications, and professional experience. I know that some of you reading this probably have pretty impressive qualifications and experience to your name that you could document.

As for myself, my qualifications, experience, and educational background are not that impressive. I am pretty good at spelling, but not always so great with commas, paragraph divisions, and sometimes grammar. As a matter of fact, while I was writing this, I had to Google how to even properly type the word *resumé* and where to put the little accent mark and how many of them to add. Wikipedia had the two accent marks on both the first and last e. It also stated that variant spellings can be with just one accent mark on the last letter as in *resumé* or no accent mark at all as in *resume*. I'm still not sure which one is correct or even if all three of them are. I like the way it looks with just one accent mark on the end, so that is what I'm going to use. If you have any special insight on this, please feel free to share it with me.

Okay, let's get back on topic. So God left us with His written resumé, if you will allow me to refer to it as that, in the Bible. His qualifications and experience are as impressive as they come. The position that He is seeking is to be on the throne of your heart. He wants to be your Lord and Savior and to have first place and priority in your life.

So let's move on to just some of His characteristics as outlined in the Bible, His resumé so to speak. As to His educational background, how does omniscient (All knowing, 1 John 3:20) work for you? Wondering if He can multitask? Well, He is also omnipotent (all powerful, Rev. 19:6, Rev. 1:8, KJV) and omnipresent (present everywhere at the same time, Ps. 139:7–10), so I'd say that those two are a big plus. How about productivity level? Well, He never gets tired and requires no breaks (Isa. 40:28). His quality of work even for difficult tasks? He is perfect (Ps. 18:30), never makes mistakes, and oh yeah, nothing is impossible with Him (Luke 1:37). He takes no sick days and never goes on vacation. How about the level of His creativity? He is *the* creator who hung the sun, the moon, and the stars, in the sky (Gen. 1, Col. 1:16). He created this planet, and He even created you (Ps. 139:13–16, Jer. 1:5). His resources are limitless (Ps. 24:1). He owns the cattle on a thousand hills and the wealth in every mine (Ps. 50:10, Hag. 2:8). He is completely sovereign and in total control. He will always tell you the truth as He cannot lie (Titus 1:2). As to His loyalty? He will never leave you nor forsake you (Deut. 31:6, Heb. 13:5).

With a resumé like that, you don't hire Him; you submit to Him and let Him take control! I close this chapter with another poem that I wrote that I feel fits well with what was just mentioned. It is sort of like a description or poetical resumé of our God and His majesty and miracles as taken from His Word. I hope and pray that you enjoy it and are encouraged by it.

He Is

He is the only righteous judge, never committing any crime.
He created the heavens and the earth, and He even created time.
He parted the Red Sea and saved Jonah from the whale,
Sent manna down from heaven and defeated the prophets of Baal.
He once made a donkey speak, much to Balaam's shock.
He made the sun stand still and brought water from a rock.
He made the walls of Jericho fall completely down
And caused the Egyptian army in the Red Sea to drown.
He protected three Hebrew children in a furnace full of fire.
He saved Daniel from the lions when the king came to inquire.
He is the Alpha and Omega, the beginning and the end.
His majesty and attributes are hard to comprehend.
He is Jehovah, Yahweh, I AM, El-Shaddai.
He is Christ, Messiah, Elohim, and Adonai.
His arrival was foretold centuries before His virgin birth.
It was prophesied by Isaiah and proclaimed to all the earth.
He healed the sick and raised the dead.
And with a single lunch 5,000 He once fed.
He walked on water, controlled the waves and the wind.
He lived this life like you and I, and yet He never sinned.
He caused the deaf to hear and the blind to see.
For you to know Him, my friend, is my earnest plea.
He is perfectly holy and cannot even look upon sin.
Had He not intervened, His forgiveness we could not win.
We all fall short of His perfect sinless standard of measure.
To have true peace with God is life's most precious treasure.
Hell has no exits and no parolees.
He is the only cure for our fallen sin disease.
Don't wait until tomorrow; it just might be too late.
Dying without the Son forever seals your fate.

Our efforts and good works are as a filthy rag.
It's not by what we do so that no one can brag.
He entered His own creation in the form of a man.
And in Jesus, God's own Son, He revealed salvation's plan.
He took your sin upon Himself and died in your stead.
Three days later, He overcame the grave and rose from the dead.
It was His love for you and I that put Him on that tree.
To offer us redemption and from the penalty of sin, be free.
By His grace and through faith, repent and believe.
There is nothing more that you can do for heaven to achieve.
Trust in Jesus, and the Holy Spirit you will receive.
He will guide you into all truth, never to deceive.
His grace is amazing, and His truth endures forever.
You will be eternally secure, and from His grasp none can sever.
He can transform your heart and make all things new.
Does the God that I've described live inside of you?

Randy Mlejnek

36

When Life Just Doesn't
Make Sense

As I sit back and reflect on all of the good things in my life, I quickly realize that I have much to be thankful for. At the end of the day yesterday, my wife and I sat down with our kids, and we all took multiple turns talking about what we were thankful for. It is so easy to find things to complain about, but what good does that do? God tells us to give thanks in all things in 1 Thessalonians 5:18. James 1:17 tells us that every good thing comes down from above from our heavenly Father.

I have my sins forgiven, a home waiting for me in heaven, a beautiful and loving wife, three precious healthy children, a good secure job, a roof over my head, food on my plate, no serious medical conditions, and I could go on. I have so many blessings! I realize however that not everyone can say those things and that my circumstances could change in the blink of an eye. If they do, may I say as Job, "though He slay me, yet will I trust in Him" (Job 13:15). There are many people that are going through difficult storms and trials in their lives, and you may be one of them. I know plenty of people who are battling cancer or that have lost loved ones to it. I know others that are struggling to make ends meet just to put food on their table.

I know some who are in a broken and abusive marriage. For you, it could be depression, stress, bitterness, anger, an addiction, a painful medical condition or injury, a broken heart, the loss of a job, the loss of a relationship, or even the loss of a loved one.

I have been through my own share of storms, trials, and struggles in my own life. I don't know exactly what yours may be, nor will I try to say that I understand what you are going through. I do realize though that life does not always make sense, and it is not always fair. Life and your current circumstances may even have you so broken to the point that you feel like you just cannot do it anymore. You may even be contemplating suicide.

May I just say that there *is* hope. Life does not always go the way we want it to or would have planned. Quite frankly, you will not truly be able to cope with the struggles of this life apart from a right relationship with your Creator. In the midst of your pain you may be asking yourself, why? The bottom of a bottle of alcohol or a handful of pills is not the answer, God is. Elisabeth Elliot once said, "Faith does not eliminate questions. Faith knows where to take them." That, my friend, is the first step, do you know Him?

I'm not asking if you are a church member, do you read the Bible, have you been baptized, did you pray some prayer in the hour of crisis, or if you simply believe in God. I'm asking if you have a personal relationship with our Lord and Savior, Jesus Christ? Have you been saved, born again, regenerated, and know it? That is where true hope is. Apart from Him, there is no hope. He is the Great Physician. He is the divine healer.

Maybe you are a Christian, but you have been running from God. I have worn those running shoes before, and it is a path I pray that I never travel down again. If this is you, won't you come back to Him today?

Like I said, life is hard, and it does not always make sense. You may actually never know this side of eternity, why things played out the way that they did. Maybe you know God and are trying to live a life that is pleasing to Him, but you just feel like the whole world is caving in on top of you. You may even feel like God has forgotten about you. Let me assure you that He has not. By faith, trust Him. Keep pressing on. Don't give up. Do not grow weary in well doing (Gal. 6:9). From our earthly human perspective, we don't always understand. His ways are higher than our ways, and His thoughts higher than our thoughts (Isa. 55:8–9). Despite what pain and heartache you may have already gone through, God is still in control, and He will work all things together for good to those who love Him and to those who are the called according to His purpose. If we put all things in God's hand, we will see God's hand in everything. I close this chapter with a poem I wrote that I pray will be an encouragement to you.

Don't Give Up

Job 14:1: "Man that is born of a woman is
of few days and full of trouble."
Pursuing things that when judged, will burn
up like wood, hay, and stubble.
Trials will come, and your faith will be tried.
Trust in His Word, and let it be your guide.
When tragedy strikes and doesn't make sense
And heartache grips you and burns so intense,
Will your foundation crumble when it's rocked to the core?
Will your anchor hold and keep you from washing ashore?
Did you build upon the sand or on Christ the solid rock?
When the winds blow, will you hold strong like a lock?
When Satan seeks to tempt you and sift you like wheat,
Will you stand strong in the Lord, or run away in retreat?
I've yet to meet a person who has not been touched by grief.
Seeking answers in the wrong places, you will find no relief.
Whether death, disease, injury, or cancer,
The Great Physician is life's only answer.
Life is like a giant cross-stitch, and we only see the backside.
Full of knots and tangled threads like only randomness was applied.
From our perspective, the pieces of the puzzle don't seem to fit.
At times, it can be overwhelming and make you want to quit.
His majesty and power none other can compare.
All your doubts and worries take to Him in prayer.
God will supply all your needs according to His riches in glory.
Rest in Him and know that this is not the end of your story.
He cares for the sparrow that falls from the tree.
How much more does He care for you and for me?
His thoughts and ways are higher than our own.
He's in complete control and still sits on the throne.

If you are carrying a burden that is hard to accept.
Remember it is okay to cry, for even Jesus wept.
God works all things together for good; just hold on and wait.
That promise can be found in the Bible in Romans 8:28.
Remain faithful, though your suffering may be hard to bear.
Rejoice knowing the Crown of Life one day you will wear.
Once in heaven, and from the troubles of life you are free,
The other side of God's tapestry you will finally get to see.
Then you will understand, not in part, but the whole.
Every thread of circumstance played a specific role.
It will reveal such a beautiful deliberate design.
Overjoyed to know that I am His, and He is mine.
What a blessed hope you have as a believer.
To one day see the work of the master weaver.

Randy Mlejnek

37

The Most Amazing
Book Ever Written

The Holy Bible is undoubtedly the greatest selling book of all time. It is also the most widely distributed book in all of history. There is no other book that has been translated into more languages than the Bible. There are millions upon countless millions of books in the world today, but only one of them was written by God Himself. If you perform just a cursory search and study common facts about the Bible, you will discover rather quickly that it is unlike any other book. I wish to highlight some of those things for you to show the uniqueness of the Bible. Many of these things have been investigated, studied, searched out, confirmed, and detailed with many sources cited by men much smarter and wiser than I.

First of all, it is a common misconception that the Bible is simply one book. It is rather a collection of sixty-six separate books. There are thirty-nine in the Old Testament and twenty-seven in the New Testament. These sixty-six books were written by about forty different authors over a period of around 1,500 years or so. Most of these writers never even knew each other, nor did they all live at the same time. The different writers came from very diverse backgrounds. There were everything from kings and military commanders to fishermen and tax collectors.

The Bible was written during different moments of human history. The writers wrote as they experienced their lives in the many ups and downs that came with it. David wrote with great sorrow and regret following his sin with Bathsheba. The apostle John wrote with great joy and wonder as he described the vision of heaven he was given. Your mood at any given time will always affect your writing. The writers of the Bible also wrote on a variety of very divisive topics.

The Bible was written on three different continents; Africa, Asia, and Europe. It was originally written in three different languages; Hebrew, Greek, and Aramaic. Yet despite all of the above, the Bible contains no historical errors! Even more amazing than that, again notwithstanding the aforementioned facts, the Bible is one complete harmonious narrative. From cover to cover, it seamlessly flows into and shares one common theme and storyline. That is nothing short of miraculous. No other book or series of books even comes close to matching that type of uniqueness and consistency in design.

There have been scores of people who have attempted to disprove the Bible or eradicate it all together. There has never been anyone who has succeeded. It is the most reliable, accurate, and trustworthy of all ancient literature. There is more manuscript evidence for the reliability of the scriptures than any other piece of ancient literature. There are over 5,500 manuscripts for the New Testament in existence today. Just to put this in perspective, the closest of the ancient writings in manuscript evidence is Homer's Iliad with 643 manuscript copies. So if a critic of the biblical writings wishes to dismiss them, they must also dismiss other ancient writings from the likes of Aristotle, Plato, or Socrates.

Time and time again, archaeological discoveries have proven the historical accuracy and cultural references mentioned in the Bible. There are also many nonbiblical sources that corroborate the Bible's narrative. The historian Josephus would be just one example. This short list contained in this chapter is certainly not exhaustive of all of the evidences for the reliability and trustworthiness of the Bible. There are many other convincing proofs that have been studied, researched, and verified. I will, however, give one more.

Probably one of the most convincing evidences of the Bible's origin being of divine design is that of prophecy. Much of the prophetic writing in scripture was a foretelling of history before it ever happened. The purpose of this predictive prophecy was to authenticate the credibility of God and, ultimately, His Word. These were not just educated guesses or coincidences that happened to come true. Some of these prophecies were recorded hundreds of years before they ever took place. They were precise in their details and timing. They came to pass with exact precision in their details and fulfillment without even the slightest of error. Over three hundred prophecies were fulfilled in Jesus Christ alone. This goes beyond mathematical possibility and any human reasoning to conclude that it was anything other than miraculous divine foreknowledge. This is one of the main things that separates the Bible from any other religious book or historical writing.

I, of course, believe that the Bible is the very inspired words of God. It makes this claim for itself in 2 Timothy 3:16. That verse tells us that all scripture is given by inspiration of God. It is literally "God breathed." So even though God used many different people to write the Bible, they wrote the very words He wanted them to record. They were under the direct influence and inspiration of the Holy Spirit. The Bible tells us in 2 Peter 1:21 that holy men of God spoke as they were moved by the Holy Ghost. I believe not only in God's inspiration of the scriptures but also that He preserved His word down through the ages for us today. I would like to close out this chapter with a poem I wrote about the Bible.

Holy Bible

Let me tell you about a book that is unlike any other.
Written about a King revealed from cover to cover.
It's never once been proven false, though many have tried.
Even the most scholarly critics have had to swallow their pride.
There are no scientific or historical errors in its pages.
Men have tried to stamp it out all through the ages.
It contains sixty-six separate books written over 1,500 years.
By 40 different authors, yet to one common storyline it adheres.
It is the ultimate truth and you can trust in it with confidence.
Written under the influence of the Holy Spirit by divine providence.
Originally written in Hebrew, Aramaic, and Greek,
Yet a complete harmony that makes it so unique.
Through prophecy, history was written
down before it ever took place.
Convincing proof that its origin came from
beyond our time and space.
It is the greatest selling book ever composed.
The very words of God Himself are enclosed.
It is quick and powerful and sharper than any two-edged sword.
By His grace, put your faith in Him, and you will have your reward.
His name is Jesus Christ, Messiah, God's only begotten son.
There is nothing more that you can do; the victory has been won.
The entire book points to His sacrifice to purchase His bride.
Will you trust in Him and His word and let it be your guide?
It explains our creation and the beginning of time.
It speaks of His holiness and His love so sublime.
It details how sin entered the human race.
Of His majesty, mercy, and amazing grace.
It tells of a rescue operation that He orchestrated to save the lost,
How He purchased our redemption and His blood was the cost,

How God entered His creation and Himself became a man,
To demonstrate His love toward us was His master plan.
He humbled Himself and experienced the torture of the cross,
Took our sin upon Himself so we wouldn't have to suffer loss.
Three days later, victoriously He arose from the dead.
That is the Gospel message, far and wide it has spread.
Only one book was ever written by God
so you wouldn't be led astray.
Will you read His words and listen to what He has to say?

Randy Mlejnek

38

The Holy Spirit

Christianity is the only religion in the world that teaches that a person's God comes and lives inside of them. I think the profoundness of this thought gets glossed over in the twenty-first century. If you have never really taken the time to dwell on the awe and wonder of this thought, I would like you to contemplate some biblical truths for a few moments. Not only does the one true living almighty God and creator of the universe truly exist (the evidence is overwhelming), but you can know about Him because He has revealed Himself in a written revelation in the Bible. His powerful, divine, miraculous, and eternal truth has been recorded, copied and providentially preserved down through the ages so that you and I could have a copy of it today.

Not only can you know *about* God, but you can also have a personal relationship with Him, made possible through His Son, Jesus Christ. The all-powerful, self-existent, eternal God humbled Himself and entered His own creation by becoming a man and taking on human flesh—all for the purpose of demonstrating His love toward us by dying for us and making a way of salvation and eternal redemption for the human race. We who were lost, dead in our trespasses and sins, were provided a way of escape unto eternal life, paid for and purchased by the blood and life of God Almighty Himself. He then proved Himself to be God and that He held power over life and death by His glorious resurrection, that through Him, we too can live again after this life, resurrected unto eternal glory in His presence.

Almost every other religious belief system is about man working his way to God, trying to appease the divine through his own efforts to bridge the gap between the created and the creator. In Christianity, God came down to man and did it all for him. God bridged the divide with the cross. In the other religions the emphasis is on *do*; in Christianity, it is on *done*!

It doesn't stop there either. Not only did God come and die for us, leave us a guidebook—a roadmap if you will—but He gives us another glorious and amazing promise as well. Not only can you know about Him, have a personal relationship with Him where you can communicate and talk with Him through prayer, but He will also come and live inside of your very body. The moment you accept Christ as your Savior and become born again, not only do you get your sins forgiven, but He also gives you His Holy Spirit. Your body literally becomes the temple of the living God (1 Cor. 6:19).

I mean this is deep and powerful stuff. God Himself will indwell you and then empower you to live for Him. He seals you, guides you, teaches you. He is omnipresent, sanctifies you, reveals Christ to you and in you, regenerates you. He brings unity to the body of Christ and empowers you to live a holy life. All the resources of heaven are at your very disposal. Yes, temptation to sin will still be there, your old sinful nature will still war against your new nature while in this earthly life. It will be a constant battle and struggle. But praise the Lord, greater is He that is in me than he that is in the world (1 John 4:4).

The third person of the trinity in the divine Godhead has many functions in the life of a believer. He convicts us of our sin (John 16:8). He is our helper and comforter (John 14:16–17), guides us into all truth (John 16:13), sanctifies us (2 Thess. 2:13), gives us true hope (Rom. 15:13, Col. 1:27), and a peace that passes all under-standing (Phil. 4:7). He seals us (Eph. 1:13–14), intercedes for us (Rom. 8:26–27), exalts and glorifies Jesus (John 16:14), comforts us (Acts 9:31), gives us spiritual gifts (1 Cor. 12:8–11), and produces fruit in our lives (Gal. 5:22-23). Those are just some of things that the Holy Spirit does for us.

The God of the Bible is one God manifested in three persons; God the Father, God the Son, and God the Holy Spirit. A bit of a mystery and a mental hurdle for our finite minds to fully compre-hend but clearly taught in the Scriptures no less. An in-depth dis-cussion and discourse on the doctrine of the trinity will have to be a topic for another day. The Holy Spirit is not just some impersonal force. He is fully God, is alive, and is a person with a will who can speak. I realize that these are some very deep spiritual truths and mental food for thought on which to chew. I wonder, however, does the God that I've described live inside of you?

I close this chapter with a poem that I wrote recently about the Holy Spirit. I pray that it will be a blessing and an encouragement to you.

The Holy Spirit

The Lord didn't give us His word to obey and
then leave us on our own to sink or swim.
You see, Christianity is the only religion where a
man's God comes to live inside of him.
God sent us His Spirit to assist us, a counsellor,
one who is called to come alongside.
All the resources of heaven are at our disposal;
He is our helper, comforter, and guide.
Jesus promised to never leave or forsake us, so
He sent one to be with us in His stead.
This One is known as the Holy Spirit; He is
the third person in the triune godhead.
Co-equal with the Father and Son, of the same
essence, but His function is unique.
He teaches, equips, and leads, but only in
accordance with God's Word will He speak.
He produces in believers fruit that is the evidence
of His work that others can plainly see.
These are listed for us in Galatians chapter five,
verses twenty-two through twenty-three
He brings unity to the body and gives to each
believer at least one spiritual gift.
He restrains evil and convicts us of our sin
when from the will of God we drift.
The Spirit gives to us everlasting life through spiritual regeneration
And begins indwelling the believer at the moment of their salvation.
Men spoke as they were carried along by the Spirit;
by His inspiration, they were stirred.
All Scripture is God breathed, so the Spirit is the
author of the Bible, God's Holy Word.

He empowers and fills, comforts and cleanses,
and into all truth, He will lead.
He helps us when we pray, and on our behalf
to the Father, He will intercede.
Our salvation is secure until the day of redemption;
by the Holy Spirit we are sealed.
One day to be resurrected, when from the curse
of sin our bodies are finally healed.
He testifies of Christ, sanctifies us, and from
the power of sin, He sets us free.
It is an amazing and personal relationship I have
with God, and He lives inside of me.

Randy Mlejnek

39

The Hardest Lesson I
Ever Had to Learn

I want to share one of the toughest lessons that I have learned in my life. Before I detail some of my experience and reveal that lesson to you, I would like to point out some things. First of all, this life lesson was already one I knew about even from a very young age. For it is detailed in the pages of the Bible, God's Holy Scriptures. A book that I have read, studied, and been instructed on from my youth. Yet I ignored the wisdom given to me and travelled down a road even though I knew deep down that it would lead to an unhappy ending. Human nature is stubborn like that. People can go through life one of two ways. They can learn from the mistakes and experiences of others who have been there and done that, or they can ignore that insight and experience and make those same mistakes for themselves. I chose the latter on more than one occasion.

The lesson that I learned was not complex in and of itself, but the process through which I went to really learn it was difficult and painful. It didn't just affect me either. My poor decisions hurt many that I love and care about. I learned a long time ago that we don't sin in a vacuum. Our decisions will impact other people. Sin has a ripple effect. It is just like throwing a rock out into the middle of a still pond. The water will ripple and spread outward from where the rock landed.

The lesson that I learned was that there is no true peace and lasting happiness in this life apart from a right relationship with the Creator of the universe. It is a peace that passes all understanding (Phil. 4:7). There is a God-shaped hole in our hearts that we unfortunately try to fill with everything but the only one who can truly fill that void. This is how we were designed and created by God, to have a relationship with Him. He gave us His Word written down and recorded in the scriptures to help us understand these truths. Many times, those words go ignored and unheeded. For some, it is material possessions; for others, it is selfish pursuits. People attempt to fill the void in their souls with all sorts of things that will ultimately leave them miserable and feeling even more empty than before. Some of these "things" include a long list of sinful vices that they abuse: sex, pornography, drugs, alcohol, food, extramarital relationships, the pursuit of wealth, power, fame, or material possessions, and the list could go on.

All these things may produce temporary happiness and satisfaction as the Bible tells us that there is pleasure in sin but only for a season (Heb. 11:25). They will, however, never truly fulfill. The sinful human appetite can never be satisfied no matter how much you indulge it. In fact, the opposite happens. The more you feed your destructive and selfish desires, the stronger they become and the more they want—in the end, only to leave you more empty than before and unsatisfied.

Worldly wisdom tells us to do whatever makes us happy. We are told that we only live once and to pursue whatever we want. If it is popular then it is right and worth doing yourself. He who dies with the most toys wins. Let your feelings and emotions be your guide. None of that is wise at all! God outlines boundaries in His Word for us to live by for a reason. He is omniscient, yet we still act like we know better than he does.

Ravi Zacharias said, "Pleasure without God, without the sacred boundaries, will actually leave you emptier than before. And this is the biblical truth, this is experiential truth. The loneliest people in the world are amongst the wealthiest and most famous who found no boundaries within which to live. That is a fact I've seen again and again."

One of the wisest men to ever walk the earth was Solomon. He was also one of the wealthiest, and had a lot of power and fame too. He spared himself no pleasure (Eccles. 2:10). He indulged in just about every pleasure and pursuit imaginable. Yet when he looked back over the course of his life and penned his journal, the book of Ecclesiastes, he said all is vanity under the sun. It was like chasing after the wind, meaninglessness. It left him emptier than before he started. G. K. Chesterton once said, "Meaninglessness does not come from being weary of pain. Meaninglessness comes from being weary of pleasure."

One of the most miserable places to be is to be a born-again child of God and then to backslide and try to live life your own way when you know better. Many people have gotten off track in this way, just look at King David in the Old Testament. The scriptures tell us that he was a man after God's own heart (Acts 13:22). Yet he allowed his sinful lusts and desires to cloud his judgment and dictate his actions. He attempted to live life his way instead of God's way. He paid a great price for that in his sin with Bathsheba too.

That is really what it all comes down to—your way or God's way. I won't get into the specifics of the many sinful choices I have made over the course of my life. I will say that the only times that I have been truly happy, satisfied, and at peace were during the times that I was surrendered to God and His will and way for my life. The other times, when I was trying to do it my way, were when I was the most miserable. Those times have come at a great cost to me and those that I love. God only knows the damage I have done to hurt my Christian testimony and reputation because of trying to live life my way. God only knows the blessings I have forfeited because of my unfaithfulness to Him at times. It is awful difficult to share your faith or sound biblical advice with someone who knows of your past faults and failures. Trying to outlive a label of hypocrisy is like trying to out run a poor diet on a treadmill. If only I would have heeded the words of Proverbs 3:5–7: "*Trust in the Lord with all thine heart; and lean not unto thine own understanding (v. 5). In all thy ways acknowledge him, and he shall direct thy paths (v. 6). Be not wise in thy own eyes; fear the Lord and depart from evil (v. 7)*" (KJV). There really is no true peace in this life outside of a right relationship with God. Romans 5:1 states, "*Therefore being justified by faith, we have peace with God through our Lord Jesus Christ*" (KJV). Are you at peace with God today? May I urge you to seek God's will and way for your life in all that you do. You are free to choose but you are not free from the consequences of those choices. You will reap what you sow. How thankful I am for a God who pursued me even when I was running from Him.

Below is a poem I wrote that I believe fits well with the topic of this chapter. I pray that it will be a blessing and an encouragement to you. God bless.

True Peace and Happiness

What is your measure of a man's success?
Material possessions or prestige to impress,
A large house, popularity, or wealth,
Friends, good looks, a clean bill of health,
The car that you drive or the clothes that you wear.
The moment you die they vanish into thin air.
All this cannot quench the thirst of your soul.
That is a void that only God can make whole.
Not sex, drugs, or a bottle of pills,
None of these things truly fulfills.
Not adultery, pornography, fornication, or lust,
Their end leads to misery, this truth you can trust.
Not whiskey, gambling, beer, or wine,
None can replace His true love divine.
Not rum, tequila, vodka, or gin,
But drink the Living Water and you will never thirst again.
Unlimited pleasure will only lead to unlimited regret,
Filled with memories that you'll wish you could forget.
Whether chasing after power, riches, or fame,
The results you get will always be the same—
A lonely emptiness that this life cannot fill.
It comes from seeking to please your own will.
You could get all your desires served on a silver platter,
But only what you do for Christ is what will truly matter.
Solomon spared himself no earthly pleasure,
Yet his can't compare to our heavenly treasure.
All of it is vanity under the sun
Like chasing the wind when all is done.
Through the playground of hedonism, you can parade around,
But only in a relationship with Jesus can true happiness be found.

Randy Mlejnek

About the Author

Randy Mlejnek is a full-time correctional officer, blogger, and Christian poet. He has been married to his wife, Amanda, since 1999, a father to three children, and a committed Christ follower. He and his wife reside in Grand Rapids, Michigan, and serve together in the children's ministry at their local church.

CPSIA information can be obtained
at www.ICGtesting.com
Printed in the USA
LVOW12s0153080617
537351LV00002B/267/P